The Birth of Merlin

OR

The Childe hath
found his Father

**Bob Stewart** is a highly respected author, composer and musician. He has written over twenty books of fiction and non-fiction, several of which feature detailed studies of the figure of Merlin taken from early sources.

**Denise Coffey** is a popular British actress and entertainer on stage, radio and television, and was associate director at The Young Vic. She has spent the last nine years directing in Canada and the USA, mainly working within the classical repertoire and specialising in plays by Shakespeare and Shaw. She has now returned to Britain to direct *The Birth of Merlin*.

**Roy Hudd** is one of Britain's best known and most popular comedian-actors. He is an authority on the history of comedy in pantomime, music hall and variety entertainment.

# The Birth of Merlin

OR

# The Childe hath found his Father

Attributed to
WILLIAM SHAKESPEARE
& WILLIAM ROWLEY

With additional chapters by R.J. Stewart,
Denise Coffey and Roy Hudd

ELEMENT BOOKS

Additional chapters © R J Stewart,
Denise Coffey, Roy Hudd 1989

Foreword © Professor Harold Brooks 1989

This edition first published in 1989 by
Element Books Limited
Longmead, Shaftesbury, Dorset

All rights reserved.
No part of this book may be reproduced or
utilised in any form or by any means,
electronic or mechanical, without
permission in writing from the Publisher.

Printed and bound in Great Britain by
Billings, Hylton Road, Worcester

Cover illustration by Miranda Gray
Cover design by Max Fairbrother

**British Library Cataloguing in Publication Data**
Shakespeare, William, *1564–1616*
 The birth of Merlin or the childe hath found his
 father. 2nd ed
 I. Title
 822.3′3

ISBN 1–85230 073–6

# Contents

**Foreword** — vii
*Professor Harold F. Brooks*

**Introduction** — 1

**The Birth of Merlin** — 3
*R.J. Stewart*

**These are the questions to ask** — 31
**— Who, When, Why, Where, How?**
*Denise Coffey*

**He may have been short, but . . .** — 55
*Roy Hudd*

**The Birth of Merlin, or** — 65
**The Childe hath Found his Father**

# FOREWORD

What gives *The Birth of Merlin* an interest which will amply justify its re-publication and a production is not any supposed link with Shakespeare, but its place in the Merlin tradition and its considerable merits, on its own account, as a play. It is fortunate to have found two editors by whose introductions these merits are so well brought out. Robert Stewart distinguishes in the tradition what is reflected in the play and what is not. Denise Coffey's analytic appreciation is particularly valuable in showing how the four strands of its plot are woven in and out, and demonstrating in it more dramatic unity than I for one had recognised.

Anyone who approaches it expecting the close knit unity and marvellously enriching cross-references of a play by Shakespeare or Jonson will of course be disappointed. The unity is of a laxer kind. But unity *is* given by the interweaving of the four strands of plot; the calculated alternations of style and tone; and the progression to a series of climaxes and a rounded-off conclusion all designed from beforehand by the dramatist. Dramatic procedures, his dramaturgy, ensure a pattern that contributes to the unity. There is much preparation: Uter, eventual successor to the throne, is given early importance by his absence, which shortly leads up to his discovery. Those old stand-bys, expectation and surprise, are turned to good account. No playgoer of any experience will fail to expect Uter's appearance.

Joan's pregnancy is an expectation in itself; the repeated inept efforts to find the child a father are pretty good earnest that the true one will be found. Modestia's rejection of her suitor is anticipated; but that by her persuasion Constantia at the altar rejects hers will come as a sensational surprise. It is also a peripety, by which what seemed to be pointing to one outcome leads to an opposite one. By Constantia's appeal, her father and bridegroom expect Modestia to be converted; but Constantia proves the convert.

Another surprise with peripety is at Artesia's first entry; Aurelius, intending to impose on the ambassadors of the defeated Saxons his unrelenting terms, is infatuated with this leader of the embassy. By a further surprise, Uter recognises in her the woman with whom he had fallen in love at first sight. His delayed entry at the beginning, hers now, and Merlin's not till midway in Act III is again a regular dramatic gambit: the delayed entry of principal persons, here the principal and second heroes, and the villainess. Merlin's advent sets going a crescendo of climaxes, with defeats of the bad in order of their importance; Proximus, Saxon magician; Vortigern, renegade Briton; the Devil who begat Merlin; the Saxon invaders, whose rout is reported; and finally the villainess Artesia, but not before her last success, the poisoning of Aurelius. This, as part of a comprehensive conclusion, brings Uter the kingship in a 'big patriotic build up' (Coffey), with Merlin's prophecy of his son Arthur's glories. Joan is provided for, with Stonehenge as her memorial, and the comic episodes reach a climax in the Clown struck temporarily dumb. Even the balked would-be husbands of Donobert's daughters are found a place as his adopted sons and heirs.

With the authority of her practical experience, Denise Coffey recognises this as an actors' play. Among the signs of that is the reliance placed upon theatre language other than dialogue: what else is heard, including music, and what is seen, including costume: the play is a notably spectacular one. Characteristic of actors' plays (though of course not confined to them) is the provision of 'turns' for pairs of actors, for example, for Uter with Artesia's gentlewoman, and then with Artesia herself; between Sir Nicodemus Nothing and the Clown; and of 'good acting parts': Merlin, Uter, Aurelius, Artesia, offering considerable range; Edol, lacking that, but forceful; Modestia; the two comics.

The actor-dramatist is strong in his sense of the need for dramatic situations at frequent intervals; many episodes are miniature dramas in themselves – the two most salient being Aurelius falling for Artesia, and the broken wedding. Stock situations abound in the actor's mind: much of his play might be seen as a cobbling of these together, though it is more skillfully done than in most dramas of this type. There are the dire threats, dispelled – perhaps by a rescuer: Merlin brought to be sacrificed; Joan delivered by him from the Devil. Artesia's false accusation of Uter is in a tradition going back to Scripture and the Classics: Potiphar's wife's against Joseph, Phaedra's against Hippolytus. Good or superior supernatural power victorious over bad or inferior (Proximus worsted by Anselm, and by Merlin), recalls Aaron and the magicians of Pharaoh, and in Elizabethan drama, Green's *Friar Bacon and Friar Bungay*, and Munday's *John a Kent and John a Cumber*. The Clown's utterance reduced, by Merlin's supernatural power, to 'hum, hum, hum' has a precedent, Robert Stewart reminds us, in the 'blerwm, blerwm' to which Taliesin reduces the bards of Maelgwn Gwynedd (and, also no doubt of traditional descent, Papageno's comic penance in *The Magic Flute*). The overhearing of Uter (II, i) is another familiar motif: one remembers its part in *Hamlet* and *Much Ado About Nothing*.

Nevertheless, as a Shakespearean, I do not believe that *The Birth of Merlin* would ever have been connected with him, but for the claim of a bookseller on the make; a claim, worthless as evidence, which Kirkman first advanced in his notoriously untrustworthy list of plays in 1661. To accept on the other hand, as is customary, the attribution to Rowley, is not unreasonable. Unlike Shakespeare's, in 1662 his name was no catchpenny. He was, as the play's author evidently must have been, an actor-dramatist; and it seems neither above nor below his talents, judging by what little we know of them. This is not a dramatist who sets one asking what his criticism of life may be. His aim is to create an effective stage-play, and in that he has succeeded. Sub-textually there is something deeper. For instance, Artesia is not unrelated to the anima archetype in its destructive aspect; Merlin to the trickster both in the mischief of the magic pick-pocketing and in his function of coming to the rescue; and he inherits from the whole Merlin tradition his character as Puer Eternus, like Taliesin: relevantly the Clown compares him (to his advantage) with Tom Thumb. But these elements of archetypal sub-text do not seem part of Rowley's conscious design: more likely to be so is the pattern of opposites to which Denise Coffey draws attention. She has faithfully reported what I said to her about the authorship.

To conclude this foreword, I shall amplify and qualify it a little. C.F. Tucker Brooke, scholarly editor of the play in *The Shakespeare Apocrypha*, believed he saw in a few passages 'a remote kinship' to Shakespeare's style. I can't detect this myself, and whether or not it exists neither Denise Coffey nor Robert Stewart, any more than I, or indeed Tucker Brooke, would dream of attributing to Shakespeare any of the writing of *The Birth of Merlin*.

Stewart is ready to find for that play and Prospero the magician a common origin in the Merlin tradition: and C.J. Sisson in his authoritative study, 'The Magic of Prospero' (*Shakespeare Survey*, Vol.II) notes one common feature: by the power of his 'stick', Prospero charms Ferdinand from moving: it is a power Merlin displays in an eminently accessible source, Malory's *Morte d'Arthur*. But whatever Prospero might owe to Merlin, the debt would only be a minor one. His whole conception and depiction (for which see both Sisson, and my British Academy lecture, *'The Tempest': What sort of play?*) are fully accounted for, apart from Merlin as a forefather. As one of the ten sovereigns or would be sovereigns in *The Tempest* he concludes a long line, going right back to the *Henry VI* plays, in which Shakespeare explores the qualifications for true sovereignty (before Prospero, only Theseus and Prince Hal qualify). His other great function is to embody, as mage no less than true sovereign, the highest to which human nature can aspire; and it is to Prospero the mage that his white magic belongs.

To retain for Shakespeare some conceivable share in the genesis of *The Birth of Merlin*, Denise Coffey makes the cautious suggestion of former talk between him and Rowley. She has every right to remark the parallel between Rowley's sensational scene of the broken wedding, and Shakespeare's in *Much Ado About Nothing*. I would add another: the Devil on stage, seen by Joan and the audience but invisible to the Clown, brings to mind the Ghost, Hamlet who sees it, and Gertrude who cannot. But I should account for these and any other resemblances in the same way as Tucker Brooke explains the 'remote kinships' he finds with Shakespeare's style: Rowley is imitating Shakespeare.

There is no difficulty in presuming so: even (which is by no means certain) if *The Birth of Merlin* is earlier than the First Folio (1623) which would have provided him with a text of all Shakespeare's plays, a sufficient number had appeared in Quarto – in particular there were good Quarto's of *Hamlet* (1604–5) and *Much Ado About Nothing* (1600) – besides what Shakespeare he might have seen in performance.

With these two suggestions of our editors – not put forward as anything more – I cannot go along. But that in no way lessens my admiration of what their introductions provide. Denise, greatly expert in the arts of the theatre, has furnished us with an enlightening exposition of the play, primarily (but not solely) from the theatrical point of view. Roberts out of his impressive mastery of the whole Merlin tradition, has put the play for us in that wide context. To both we are warmly grateful.

*Professor Harold F. Brooks*

# INTRODUCTION

When I heard of the existence of the *The Birth of Merlin* some years ago, it seemed merely a curiosity, one of the Shakespeare apocrypha which was certainly no concern of mine. But in insinuating ways the play reminded me of its existence: between my first hearing of it and ignoring it in the mid 1970s, and 1985 when a copy came into my possession, I had written a number of books on Merlin and related subjects. As these were gradually published between 1984 and 1988, and the highly recondite, obscure but entertaining annual *Merlin Conference* made sail in London, with myself lashed to the rudder, so did the play inexorably surface.

John Matthews, my occasional co-writer, who has the good fortune to be a librarian as well, sent me a facsimile copy published by the Tudor Text Society in the late nineteenth century: some time after this I received several letters from Patricia Villiers-Stuart, who, not knowing of the facsimile edition, had undertaken the daunting task of making a handwritten copy from an early edition in the British Museum.

Having worked with director Denise Coffey on several theatre productions, I asked John Matthews to send her a further copy of the facsimile, and at around the same time I published two scenes from the play in the first *Book of Merlin* (Blandford Press, 1986), a more or less annual anthology that grew from the Conferences, along with many other Merlinesque matters by various contributors. In the same volume I also published, for the first time in this century, a remarkable dissertation on the nature of Merlin as a prophet written by Thomas Heywood in 1641, as part of his *Chronographical History* or *Life of Merlin Ambrosius*. This fascinating book has now been republished entire by Jones (Wales) Publishers, though their facsimile of the 1812 edition does not, regrettably, state that the original book was first published in 1641, or tell us anything about Thomas Heywood, who was an author and playwright of some breadth.

When I first read *The Birth of Merlin or The Childe hath found his Father*, I was slightly disappointed. I had expected something more immediately mystical and serious (perhaps similar to, dare I say it, *The Tempest*?), with more of Merlin and less of his Mum and Nuncle. But that was because I was so overstuffed with Merlinic lore from my deadly serious researches into Geoffrey of Monmouth's texts, that I was unable to digest and assimilate the nourishing mixture of comedy, spectacle, magic, and spiritual endeavour that *The Birth of Merlin* offers.

I must acknowledge, therefore, that Denise Coffey, who read the play as a director, first steered me through the text as it might work on stage.

From that point, I began to appreciate the rollicking humour, the themes of marriage and chastity, spirituality and sensuality, and to grasp that this script would be very powerful and highly entertaining when translated into action. Clearly it was written by someone who was well versed in performance, and it was not a mere curiosity to be unearthed only for its unconfirmed claim to have been co-written by William Shakespeare.

But as I became more familiar with the text, preparing it, with Denise, for performance and for entire publication in this new edition, and composing music, with Stuart Gordon, for the first major British production since the days of William Rowley, I had a number of further realisations concerning *The Birth of Merlin*. These are in my chapter on the play which follows, but the most interesting are worth summarising briefly at this stage.

Despite the liberal bawdy comedy, the character of Merlin himself, even when portrayed as a Hairy Artichoke, remains inviolate. He shows exactly the same attributes in this 1620 play as he does in the 1235 (or thereabouts) works of Geoffrey of Monmouth, who wrote down and elaborated upon traditional Celtic lore concerning Merlin preserved by Welsh and Breton bards or story-tellers. This is more remarkable than you might think, for this primal Merlin is *not* a wise old man who waves wands and protects King Arthur – for that Merlin is a literary invention.

The original Merlin was a child prophet, offspring of a maiden and a mysterious spirit. He predicted the coming of Arthur, helped with his begetting, and carried him, mortally wounded, to the Otherworld for his cure – but was not present during Arthur's glorious career. Furthermore, Merlin was entirely good – not fighting a struggle between diabolical forces within himself and his human nature; but admittedly his good qualities were those of a culture and spiritual vision far removed from that of the present day. This innate mystery and spiritual power is clear in our play; although his father is the Devil 'with his head horrid', Merlin is not diabolical, and always works actively against evil and corruption when he is faced with it, though he is never a crusader or evangeliser. How could he be, as he was never a Christian?

*R. J. Stewart*
*Bath, 1989*

# THE BIRTH OF MERLIN
## *R. J. Stewart*

The chapter which follows has been carefully confined to the legendary and magical motifs, themes and characters within *The Birth of Merlin*; certain related subjects and persons are, in context, inevitable, and I make no excuse for their appearance. There is no attempt here to trace the literary development of the play, though most of the characters can be found, in various guises, simply by reading Geoffrey of Monmouth's *History of the Kings of Britain* in any of the excellent translations and editions available. I have instead concentrated upon the character of Merlin, the presence (and absence) of magical traditions in the text, and some of the more obscure but important connections to sixteenth- and seventeenth-century attitudes to magic, folklore, British legends, and their appearance in *The Tempest*, Heywood's *Life of Merlin*, and the life and works of Doctor John Dee. To travel further proved impossible in the limited vehicle of one chapter.

### The Comet and the New King

While these things were happening at Winchester [i.e. the poisoning of King Aurelius, brother of Uther Pendragon] there appeared a star of great magnitude and brilliance, with a single beam shining from it. At the end of this beam was a ball of fire, spread out in the shape of a dragon. From the dragon's mouth spread forth two rays of light, one of which seemed to extend its length beyond the latitude of Gaul, while the second turned towards the Irish Sea and split up into seven smaller shafts of light. The star appeared three times, and all who saw it were struck with fear and wonder (From Geoffrey of Monmouth's *History of the Kings of Britain* translated by Lewis Thorpe, Penguin Classics, 1966. Hereafter referred to as H.K.B.)

Charles I came to the throne, according to Heywood's *Chronographical History* (1641), on Sunday 27 March 1625. As early as 1613 William Rowley had been a popular actor in the company known as the Prince of Wales' Men, and it seems likely that some of the elements of *The Birth of Merlin* mark the transition of rule from James to Charles. The prevailing atmosphere towards the close of James' reign, in mercurial London at any rate, was one of increasing and fashionable interest in chivalry, including the revival of tilting or jousting and related spectacles. Thus the 'Matter of Britain', chivalry, kingship, and the increase in power and might of a true royal lineage were all topical and important subjects. The appearance of Arthur might be likened, if only indirectly, to the person of Charles, first as Prince of Wales, then as King.

Another interesting parallel between the chronicled history of Britain and the early seventeenth century, which must have caused considerable curiosity, panic, and wonder, was the appearance of a comet on Wednesday 18 November 1618. The appearance of blazing stars forms a major part of prophetic imagery connected to kingship and far-reaching spiritual forces of transformation; there are, of course, the important biblical motifs of the Star of Bethlehem and the stellar vision in the Book of Revelation in Christian mythology. Early Merlin texts repeatedly employ the appearance of a blazing star or comet to herald the impending birth of King Arthur, and the sight of stellar phenomena is found on several occasions in Merlin's visions as described in the medieval texts by Geoffrey of Monmouth.

> The malignity of the star Saturn shall fall down as rain, and slay mankind with a crooked sickle. The Twelve Houses of the Stars shall lament the irregular excursions of their inmates [from Geoffrey of Monmouth's *The Prophecies of Merlin* translated by J. A. Giles, quoted in R. J. Stewart, *The Prophetic Vision of Merlin*, Penguin Arkana, 1986. Hereafter referred to as P.V.M.].

> Build me a remote building with seventy doors and seventy windows through which I may watch fire-breathing Phoebus and Venus and the stars gliding from the heavens by night, all of whom shall show me what is going to happen to the people of the kingdom [from Geoffrey of Monmouth's *Vita Merlini* translated by J. J. Parry, quoted in R. J. Stewart, *The Mystic Life of Merlin*, Penguin Arkana, 1986. Hereafter referred to as M.L.M.].

> From the top of a lofty mountain the prophet was regarding the courses of the stars, speaking to himself out in the open air. 'What does this ray of Mars mean? Does its fresh redness mean that one king is dead and that there shall be another? So I see it, for Constantine has died and his nephew Conan, through an evil fate and the murder of his uncle, has taken the crown and is king. And you, highest Venus, who slipping along within your

ordered limits beneath the Zodiac and accompanying the sun in his course, what about this double ray of yours that is cleaving the air . . . ?' [M.L.M.]

Little wonder, therefore, that the appearance of a blazing star and dragons forms the concluding spectacle of *The Birth of Merlin*, written around 1620. The comet seen in 1618 might have been understood to herald, among many other superstitious or portentous things, the possible death of James and the succession of Charles. By the time the play was performed in the early years of Charles' reign, the symbolism would have been quite clear to the audience.

The spectacular elements of our play correspond, to a certain extent, to the atmosphere of the period, though many items might still have been daring and controversial. The battle scene, between Saxons and Britons, apart from being standard and well-established theatrical fare by this time, echoes the courtly interest in matters of chivalry or ancient warfare. The main spectacles, however, are magical, involving the struggle of good against evil.

It is interesting to see that King James' extreme antipathy to matters magical did not, apparently, affect *The Birth of Merlin*. It may have been acceptable because of the extremely precise role of Merlin; his spiritual nature wins over potential temptation and evil, and the Devil is banished and imprisoned.

We might also presume, without being too wildly imaginative, that the late years of James and the early years of Charles upon the throne, may have seen a mild revival of that great and dangerous interest in occult or esoteric arts that permeated the reign of Elizabeth I, or at least a lessening of persecution under the infamous Witchcraft Act.

Many of the guiding stars in that bright universe of Renaissance arts and sciences were dead, but a few still lingered on. Old Dr John Dee, the great Elizabethan scientist, mathematician, astrologer, and magician, had been, so to speak, exiled to the post of Warden of Manchester College in 1596 by Elizabeth, and no longer enjoyed active royal favour. James came to the throne in 1603, and was certainly not a monarch to take magical matters lightly, as was clearly seen by his convoluted and terrible work *Demonologie*.

Dee died in December of 1608, two years after William Shakespeare had written *Macbeth* to satisfy simultaneously the King's hatred of witches and the claim of the Stuart dynasty to the throne of Scotland. Two years before *Macbeth* was penned, in 1604, Dee had petitioned King and Parliament to clear his name, which was in general disrepute due to the royal attitude to magic, and the notorious Witchcraft Act of 27 March of the same year. His fervent and idealistic petition revolved around the fact that he had been called 'an invocator of divels', and Dee declared that he was ready to face death by stoning, live burial or burning 'if by any due, true, and just means, the name of conjurer, or caller, or invocator of Divels or dammne Sprites, can be proved to have beene to be duely or justly reported of him'. This petition was simply ignored, and no response of any kind seems to have been made. The learned and aged Doctor followed his main document with an appeal in doggerel verse:

TO THE HONOURABLE ASSEMBLIE OF THE COMMONS IN<br>THE PRESENT PARLIAMENT

> The Honor due unto you all,
> And reverence to you each one,
> I do first yeeld most speciall;
> Grant me this time to hear my mone.
>
> Now (if you write) full well you may,
> Fowle sclandrous tongues and divelish hate,
> And help the truth to bear some sway
> In just defence of a good Name.
>
> In sundry sorts, this sclander great
> Of *conjurer* I have sore blamde:
> But wilfull, rash, and spiteful heat,
> Doth nothing cease to be enflamde.
>
> Your help, therefore, by Wisdom's lore,
> And by your Powre, so great and sure,
> I humbly crave that never more
> This hellish wound I shall endure.
>
> And so your Act, with Honour great
> All ages will hereafter prayse;
> And Truth, that sitts in Heavenly seat,
> Will in like case you comforts rayse.

Most dutifully and in all humilities at your commandment, John Dee, servant and Mathematician to his most royal Majesty. Anno 1604. Junij 8.

The Act referred to in the last stanza was an Act for Suppressing Slander, which Dee, somewhat naively, requested Parliament to pass, primarily and with specific reference to himself. Dee's skill as a poet was, as may be deduced from the above example, somewhat below his better-known abilities as mathematician, navigator, and researcher into esoteric arts and sciences!

Despite the ignored petition and the final versified plea for attention, we know today that Dee was indeed involved in the invocation of spirits for many years, and some of his lengthy and detailed secret papers on this subject may still be seen in the British Museum.[1] Dee would have vigorously asserted, if his secret arts had ever been made known in detail during his lifetime, that his invocations were angelic, and always under the governance of God Almighty.

The cunning or observant reader may have noticed a connection between Dee's rather sad petition, made in the late evening of his life, and certain events in *The Birth of Merlin*. Dee requested to be *stoned, buried alive, or burnt* if any proof could be confirmed that he was a 'conjurer of divels or sprites'. Proximus is stoned to death magically by Merlin, while the Devil (or should it be Divel?) is buried alive within a great rock. Could the writer have been playfully referring to Dee's petition of some years earlier? Or were these simply references, in both Dee and Rowley, to the barbaric punishments inflicted upon deluded people in the name of religion? Was there perhaps a running sequence of jokes concerning Dee's slightly ludicrous attempt to sway Parliament during the very heat of the persecution of witches and conjurers? I leave this coincidence to the reader's judgement.

## Magic, Science, and *The Birth of Merlin*

*The Birth of Merlin* contains a number of spectacular scenes involving apparitions, visions, magical battles, and mysterious beings. It is significant that Merlin himself has his power naturally; he is born with it, and merely has to decide which path to follow, good or evil. Indeed Merlin is not a magician in our play, just as (contrary to popular belief) he is not a magician in early chronicle sources such as Nennius or Geoffrey of Monmouth.

Merlin not a magician? Not a magician but a *prophet*; this is made quite clear in early Merlin texts, and embellishments of art-magic were added by later writers, improving, as they thought, upon the collective British traditions preserved in chronicles or popular tales. In Geoffrey's *History of the Kings of Britain* Merlin utters the staggering *Prophecies*, which are likely to be a traditional set of obscure verses or utterances probably Welsh or Breton in origin, such as were mentioned but not quoted in full by Gerald of Wales in 1188: 'There I myself, Archdeacon of St Davids, discovered the [prophetic] works of Merlin Silvester, which I had long been looking for, or so I would like you to think [from *The Journey through Wales* translated by Lewis Thorpe, Penguin Classics, 1978]. Gerald mentions Welsh prophetic frenzy, the origin, name, and nature of Merlin, and various comparisons between Celtic and biblical prophecy.

Merlin does not, however, study magical arts and make spells in the earlier texts which provided sources for the later literary expansion of his character. But what about the famous transformation of Uther Pendragon into the likeness of Gorlois of Cornwall? Was this not magic to enable the begetting of King Arthur upon the lovely Ygraine? No: if we read Geoffrey carefully we find that Uther was transformed by the use of stage make-up, cosmetics, or, as Lewis Thorpe renders the term, 'drugs'.

> 'If you are to have your wish [said Merlin to Uther] you must make use of methods which are quite new and until now unheard of in your day. By my drugs I know how to give you the precise appearance of Gorlois, so that you will resemble him in every respect' [H.K.B.].

In Geoffrey's *Vita Merlini* Merlin even rejects his prophetic powers, handing the mantle to his sister Ganieda, and he seeks higher spiritual enlightenment.

> Ganieda too was at times elevated by the spirit, so that she often prophesied to her friends concerning the future of the kingdom . . .' The Boar of Brittany, protected by an aged oak, takes away the moon, brandishing swords behind her back. I see two stars engaging in combat with wild beasts beneath the hill of Urien . . .' She did not stop with this and her companions wondered at her, and her brother spoke . . . 'Sister does the spirit wish you to foretell future things since he has closed up my mouth and my book? Therefore this task is given to you, rejoice in it' [M.L.M.].

This passage employs two important traditional images also used in Rowley's *Birth of Merlin*, and which were part of the stock of images employed by traditional story-tellers (or in Geoffrey's day by bards). These are, of course, the closing up of the mouth and the closing of a book of wisdom. The stopping of speech also occurs in the Welsh legend of Taliesin, in which a miraculous prophetic child, Taliesin the primal poet, causes the dull advisers and false poets at a royal court to utter only *blwrm, blwrm,* which is the infantile sound made through sealed lips agitated by fingers.

The theme of growing beyond mere or rough magic is developed at great length in *The Tempest*, a play which seems to draw upon several Celtic and European mystical, magical, and philosophical traditions that are also found in the medieval *Vita Merlini*. So the inherent or original character of Merlin is not quite as we are led to believe by relatively modern fiction, and our play, *The Birth of Merlin* tends to uphold an older tradition of Merlin, albeit in a manner suitable for a sensational stage production. The youthful Merlin, his foolish uncle and lascivious mother, however, owe as much to Mummers' Plays and folk ritual, as they do to literature, and we shall return to this connection at a later stage.

**Polarity and Magic**

Running through the play we find a major theme of *polarity* or comparison and conflict of polar opposites; this is well constructed and maintained, and, incidentally, helps the modern audience or reader to relate to the rather difficult theme of spiritual chastity versus marital bliss. Indeed, we might doubt if the audience of the early seventeenth century, particularly Rowley's audience, were particularly attuned to the worth of chastity, but it forms part of the interwoven pattern within which the characters interact. This is a typically *magical* pattern, for magic is an artistic science connected to polarities of sexual, mental and emotional energy and the forces and potential forms of the imagination.

The saintly Hermit opposes the lascivious Artesia, and her magician Proximus. The semi-human semi-demon (originally semi-*daemon*) Merlin opposes Proximus to get in training, but soon disposes of him and battles with his own father, the Devil. The various love themes balance one another, ranging from the false love between Aurelius and Artesia to the unrequited love of Cador and Edwin. Joan Go-too't is likewise seeking her anonymous lover, to make a balanced family for her bastard child, who is currently being 'fostered' by her brother, standing in for the mysterious father.

But within this web of polarity and power, we find that Merlin does all from his inner nature. He does not train as a magician, although he is a precocious reader; he simply does what comes naturally to him. When his better spiritual nature finally triumphs, his mother Joan also undergoes a transformation, and utters sudden beautiful poetry. Detailed magic, however, or conjuration and invocation of divels, as John Dee would have said, is left to Proximus the Saxon necromancer, and is shown to be less in value and nature than the spiritual power of the holy hermit, and, more important in our present context, less than that of Merlin.

Proximus replaces, single-handed, the array of astrologers and magicians that surround King Vortigern in the *History of the King of Britain* and related chronicles, and most specifically he is related to one *Maugantius* the black magician who advises Vortigern that he must sacrifice a child born of no known father and use the child's blood to slake the mortar for building his tower. (H.K.B.)

Where does Dr John Dee fit into this web of theatrical magical forces? During the reign of Elizabeth, Dee was an eminent scientific cartographer and geographer, who fused his mathematics with a knowledge of Celtic lore, in order to lay claim to the Americas, or Atlantis as he called the vast mysterious territories to the far west. But Dee was also the magician *par excellence* of the period, frequently harassed by popular superstition and hatred, possibly serving Elizabeth as a secret agent in Europe, certainly drawing astrological charts for her, and on one occasion protecting her from a presumed malevolent spell which had been discovered lying where she might walk.

But by the time of James, as we saw above, Dee had fallen into disrepute, pensioned off to Manchester a few years earlier by Elizabeth, and not even meriting attention for his brave and foolhardy attempts to declare accusations of sorcery to be 'sclandrous'. We have noted that there is similarity, perhaps coincidental, perhaps witty, between details of Dee's petition and the fate of both Proximus and the Devil, both of whom certainly are invocators of divels.

Yet the scene of the battling spirits in *The Birth of Merlin* is typical of the type of incantation and spirit presence associated with Dee and other Renaissance magicians. It was, perhaps, a daring presentation to make, and would have been most spectacular, though we do not know how it was arranged.

In his youth, long before the *Birth of Merlin* was written, the brilliant young Dee became a fellow of the newly founded Trinity College at Cambridge, where he was under-Reader in Greek. He had been accused of black arts for making a flying beetle as a prop for a play by Aristophanes, for his skill in mechanical matters seemed unnatural to the suspicious academics. By the reign of Charles I, however, increasingly successful mechanical contrivances were beginning to appear, and the vision of a star or comet in *The Birth of Merlin* would have been a delight for an adept such as Dee to devise and enable – but, alas, he was already dead.

The playwright(s) could justifiably include shadowy spells and beings, for such phantoms were ultimately defeated by the forces of good, even to the extent of Merlin taking the side of the angels. But it is to two spirits that I would draw the reader's attention particularly, *Armel* and *Plesgeth*.

These are typical names for spirits such as are found in the Grimoires of medieval and Renaissance magic. Such texts were of course strictly illegal, yet a considerable amount of attention was given to them by learned men, and many of the leading scientists and mathematicians of the period were, inevitably, magicians and astrologers.

Dee conjured spirits with long lists of both orthodox and highly unorthodox angelic names, and his seer or scryer Edward Kelly claimed to have had communication with ranks of ethereal beings who confided their names to him. On Dee's magical emblem or seal *Sigillum Aemaeth*, which may still be seen in the British Museum, various angelic, spirit, and divine names are inscribed; *Aemeth* is derived from Hebrew *Emeth*, a word of power or Name, meaning simply 'truth'. The names include *Iana, Akele, Azdobn, Stimcul, El, Heeoa, Ath, Beigia, Hagonel, Dmal, Esemili, Madimi*, and many more. Madimi was the name of a pleasant young female spirit who advised Dee through visions seen in crystal and Edward Kelly. Some months after her first appearance, Dee named his newly born daughter Madimi; this episode is resonant of the ancient magical tradition, of which Merlin's birth is but one prime example, wherein a mysterious being from another dimension or world associates with humans in such a way that incarnation may occur.

Although I have repeatedly referred to Dee, his role in Elizabethan science, astrology, cartography and mathematics, and his possible link to certain aspects of both *The Tempest* and *The Birth of Merlin* in this chapter, there are many other writers from the period that would have been accessible, or at least notorious. *The Arbatel of Magic*, translated by Robert Turner, 1655; *The Pseudomarchia Daemonum* by Johannes Wierus, 1563, which later appeared in Reginald Scot's *Discoverie of Witchcraft*, 1584, are typical examples. Scot's book was one of the particular targets of King James' hatred of witchcraft.

It seems that Rowley's audience would have recognised spirit names, not only from orthodox religious prohibitions and the recent witchcraft persecutions, but on the more specific level suggested by *Armel* and *Plesgeth*. (As I could not find these particular spirits listed in the well-known grimoires available in modern publication, I must accept Denise Coffey's suggestion that they are, of course, fake names. Why? Because no professional actor or company will willingly risk uttering magical spells on stage, such as seems to happen in a certain Scottish play by William Shakespeare.) And in any case, were not such invocations banned by law?

**Merlin: his Nature and Character**

From at least as early as the twelfth century, comparisons have been made between Merlin and Jesus; these eventually crystallised as overt propaganda, declaring Merlin to be a type of Anti-Christ in which British (Celtic) tradition wickedly anticipated Christian revelation and mocked it with a pretence to similar attributes in the life of a central character, Merlin himself. The roots of the Merlin legends, however, may be traced to an understated protean and ancient tradition deriving from a pre-Christian era, which became absorbed into various Merlin texts from oral sources. These anonymous sources for motifs and symbolism relating to Merlin may be traced to Celtic pagan religion, which contained a central theme of human sacrifice preserving the sanctity and power of a sacred Land, personified by a goddess of Sovereignty.

There are faint echoes of this pagan religious concept in our play, deriving from various folk dramas and rituals which involve a Fool, a curious lascivious man/woman, a wise man, and the devil. Possibly such folk rituals are the last relic of the religious mystery plays of the pagan Britons. It hardly needs to be added that there were many aspects of Elizabeth's reign which resonated to the ancient tone of Sovereignty and the sacred Land.

Such themes were at first adapted and absorbed without immense conflict by the early Celtic Church, and soon became attached to various saints, many of whom had but recently been druids, prophets, or even Celtic gods and goddesses![2] Indeed, it would not have been possible in the earliest stages of incoming Christianity to strip the ancient native beliefs from the people instantly; and the remnants of genuine folk tradition preserve some pagan rituals and images even today in the age of computers and atomic weapons.

The Scottish Merlin, for example, also called Lailoken, actually undergoes a sacrificial death, but his life story is closely connected to that of the great Saint Kentigern. The prophet Lailoken, also called Merlin, is driven mad by grief at a great battle (this tradition is employed by Geoffrey to open the *Vita Merlini*), and utters prophetic insights. Close to death, he asks Saint Kentigern for the sacrament, yet also predicts that his own impending death will be in the form of stoning, impalement and drowning. True to his vision, he is killed in this triple manner by a revengeful mob of local (pagan) shepherds. A similar plot is associated with King

Suibhne, in Irish legend. Unfortunate Suibhne is cursed by the powerful Christian saint Ronan, and goes mad during a battle; he flits around Ireland living on watercress and spring water. He is finally caught, and shriven by Saint Moling, but dies from a bitter spear blow, cast by a jealous husband who mistakenly suspects the madman of adultery.

In such examples, pagan lore is fused with Christian, and the concept of an Anti-Christ or evil element to Merlin is absent. In Geoffrey of Monmouth's work, Merlin is not at any time described as evil, corrupt, or any type of Anti-Christ. The pagan theme of sacrificial death (shared by Christianity of course), is neatly moved away from the adult Merlin in Geoffrey's *Vita Merlini* and placed upon an anonymous Youth of Three Disguises. This mysterious persona is found in various forms in world mythology, as is the Fool; sometimes they are one and the same.

The youth, in the *Vita*, appears first as himself, next in disguise, and finally disguised as a woman. Merlin predicts three separate deaths for him, as a result of each of the three guises. Eventually the youth grows to manhood and suffers a Threefold Death from falling, hanging and drowning. In the Scottish legend of Lailoken/Merlin, a similar death is suffered by Merlin himself. It would have been too risky, perhaps, for Geoffrey to use this well-established tradition directly, as he was a member of both the Church and the ruling Norman minority class of his day. In any case he carried Merlin through various further adventures to live to an astonishing old age, retiring to contemplate the spiritual nature of the universe.

> There was in the hall a certain boy, one of many, and the ingenious queen, catching sight of him straightway, thought of a novel trick by which she might convict her brother [Merlin] of falsehood. So she ordered the boy to come and asked Merlin to predict what death the lad might die. Merlin answered 'Dearest sister, he shall die, when a man, by falling from a high rock.' Smiling at these words, she ordered the boy to go away and take off the clothes he was wearing and put on others, and to cut off his long hair. She bade him come back thus that he might seem to them a different person. The boy obeyed her, for he came back to them with his clothes changed as he had been ordered to do. Soon the queen asked her brother again, 'Tell your dear sister what the death of *this* boy will be like.' Merlin answered, 'This boy when he grows up shall, while out of his mind, meet with a violent death in a tree' . . . She then told the boy to go out and put on woman's clothing, and to come back thus dressed. Soon the boy left and did as he

was bid, for he came back in woman's clothes just as though he were a woman, and he stood in front of Merlin to whom the queen said, banteringly, 'Say brother, tell me about the death of this girl.' 'Girl or not, she shall die in the river!' said her brother to her, which made King Rhydderch laugh at Merlin's reasoning, since when asked about the death of a single boy he had predicted three different kinds . . .

For long years his prediction seemed to be an empty one, until the time when the boy grew to manhood; then it was made apparent to all and convincing to many. For while the youth was out hunting with his dogs he caught sight of a stag hiding in a grove of trees; he loosed the dogs, who, as soon as they saw the stag, climbed through unfrequented ways, and filled the air with their baying. He urged on his horse with his spurs, and followed after . . . There was a high mountain surrounded on all sides by rocks with a stream flowing through the plain at its foot; thither the animal fled until he came to a river, seeking a hiding place after the usual manner of its kind. The young man pressed on and passed straight over the mountain, hunting for the stag among the rocks lying about. Meanwhile it happened, while his impetuosity was leading him on, that his horse slipped from a high rock and he fell over a precipice into the river, but so that one of his feet caught in a tree, and the rest of his body was submerged in a stream. Thus he fell, and was drowned, and hung from a tree, and by this Threefold Death made Merlin a true prophet. (M.L.M.)

The story of the triple death is also found in the Welsh *Mabinogi* of *Math son of Mathonwy* in which the hero Llew is tricked into a situation whereby his rival lover can kill him under ritualised multiple circumstances. The same theme appears in Irish legend, in the story of *Da Derga's Hostel*, and played an important role in the sacrificial foundations of religion in the western world. It has its parallels, of course, in the orthodox Christian myth of the Crucifixion.

The method by which Merlin describes his great age in the *Vita* is reminiscent of a sequence of totem animals found in the *Mabinogi* of *Kuhlwch and Olwen* in which a succession of increasingly ancient beasts lead a band of heroes to their goal, the lost divine child *Mabon*. That Mabon and the young Merlin have a great deal in common is certain, but we have no space to enter into this ramification of the Merlin legends here.[3]

'In that wood there stands an oak in its hoary strength which old age, that consumes everything, has so wasted away that it lacks sap and decays inwardly. I saw this oak when it first began to grow and I even saw the acorn fall from which it came, and a woodpecker standing over it watching the branch . . .' (M.L.M.)

The emblem of a youth disguised, climbing to the hilltops with his dog or hound, and falling from a height to a mysterious death, is found in the Renaissance period in the tarot trumps of The Fool and The Hanged Man. The first is an innocent or ignorant persona who stands for all humanity, and is sometimes shown as a boy in ragged girl's clothing, while the second is a young man hanging upside down suspended from a tree, with his head in a river. Although details vary from deck to deck, the two trumps are presumably derived from the same legendary tradition that advised Geoffrey of Monmouth when he related his story of Merlin, the Youth of Three Disguises, and the Triple Death. These themes reappear in our play. *The Birth of Merlin* in an attenuated but clear form, revolving around the nature of Merlin himself as a central character.

Let us consider, briefly, a typical comparison between the attributes of Merlin from medieval legend, most specifically those set out by Geoffrey in his *History*, *Prophecies*, and *Vita*, though by no means exclusive or original to those texts, and those of Jesus as accepted in orthodox religion. We can then discover how these attributes resurface in a confused but recognisable form in our play. The attributes are set out in order broadly corresponding to the life history of Merlin as developed through the *History*, *Prophecies*, and *Vita Merlin*.

## Merlin

1. Born of a royal Maiden and a mysterious spirit (H.K.B.)
2. Has an accusatory playmate or 'brother', Dinabutius, who reveals his mysterious origins to the searching soldiers of King Vortigern. (H.K.B.)
3. King Vortigern tries to sacrifice the child Merlin and use his blood to bind the mortar of a tower which is perpetually destroyed as it is built up. This image of a false or falling tower is found in the Renaissance tarot card of The Blasted Tower, where a similar allegorical meaning of pride, misplaced power, and false aspirations is attached to it. The image is also connected to the biblical tradition of the Tower of Babel, which has a similar allegorical meaning. The Tower is, in fact, a folkloric motif occurring in a number of tales, and is used also as a multifold symbol in esoteric or magical tuition. (H.K.B.)

> 4. Confronts the false court magicians and confounds them. (H.K.B.)
> 5. Makes oracular announcements, discovering Two Dragons concealed in an underground chamber beneath the hilltop upon which the Tower is built. (H.K.B. and P.V.M.) The Dragons also appear in the Welsh *Mabonigi* of *Lludd and Llevelys*, where they are laid to rest in the centre of the land of Britain through the skill of a rightful king and his brother.
> 6. Retires to the wildwood through madness, grief and compassion, after a great battle in which many of his companions are massacred. (M.L.M.)
> 7. Is tempted by *King Rhydderch* (the husband of Merlin's sister *Ganieda*) with the rich gifts of the world. (M.L.M.)
> 8. Is associated with an ancient theme of sacrificial death, through the Threefold Death, either by predicting the death for a youth, or in some cases undergoing it himself. (*Merlin Legends* and M.L.M.)

**Jesus**

> 1. Born of a Virgin of Royal Lineage and the Holy Spirit.
> 2. (Eventually betrayed by his 'brother' Judas Iscariot.)
> 3. King Herod seeks to kill the infant through his Massacre of the Innocents, intending to keep the royal lineage within his own power.
> 4. Confronts (a) the Elders in the Temple as a youth, and (b) the money-lenders and corrupt elements associated with the Temple as a young man.
> 5. Makes oracular announcements and paradoxical teachings.
> 6. Retires to the desert to meditate.
> 7. Is tempted by Satan with rulership of the world.
> 8. Is crucified.

A number of further parallels might be added, such as the important theme of miraculous cures, which runs through the lives of both Merlin and Jesus, but these miracles do not appear in our play.

**Merlin in *The Birth of Merlin***

> 1. Is born of a bawdy Englishwoman and the Devil.
> 2. (Has an attendant spirit, possibly an echo of the twin brother theme.) The attendant spirit is also implied in Geoffrey's *History*

when Merlin refused to prophesy idly 'lest the spirit which advise me departs from me' (H.K.B.), but it is not clear if this refers to (a) an actual entity, (b) his *daemon* father, or (c) the essence or spirit of prophetic power inherent within himself. We should note that the twin brother theme is of major importance in certain Celtic myths, although it becomes vague and confused in the medieval Merlin legends.

3. Attends the court of King Vortigern, as in the *History*.
4. Confronts Proximus the Saxon magician and eventually kills him after a magical contest. Proximus is derived from one Maugantius in the *History*, who advises the blood sacrifice of a youth born of no father, to enable Vortigern to keep his tower standing.
5. Makes the traditional oracular announcements found in the *History* and elsewhere. These may be compared with those printed in Thomas Heywood's *Chronographical History* or *Life of Merlin* published in 1641. Heywood's book, incidentally, bears no relationship at all to the *Vita Merlini*, as we might think from the title, but is drawn from various chronicles and histories extant at the time of his writing. It does, however, contain some metrical prophecies and historical or pseudo-historical scenes that seem to be derived from *The Prophecies of Merlin*, and should be considered in the light of the *The Birth of Merlin* as a more or less contemporary work by an author who might have associated with William Rowley.
6. May be paralleled by his rapid development to adulthood and his love of study.
7. Is tempted by his father the Devil and defeats him, imprisoning him within in the Underworld.
8. Is not sacrificed.

In the *Vita Merlini*, the aged Merlin retires to a special observatory with three selected companions, to enter a life of spiritual contemplation of the higher mysteries of Divinity. The Threefold Death, in this variant, has been undertaken by an anonymous youth, and Merlin refuses to be a judge or druid and lead the British princes.

> 'Young men, my time of life drawing on toward old age, and so possessing my limbs that with my weakened vigour I can scarce pass through the fields, do not ask this of me . . . Nothing can tear me away from my forest of Calidon which in my opinion is always pleasant. Here shall I remain while I live, content

with apples and grasses, and I shall purify my body with pious fastings that I may be worthy to partake of the life everlasting' [M.L.M.].

In *The Birth of Merlin*, Merlin constructs Stonehenge as a memorial for his mother Joan, and though the connection between Merlin and Stonehenge is well-established in early chronicles, the dedication to his mother is unique to our play. Geoffrey develops the Stonehenge tradition in the *Vita* by turning it into a special observatory built for Merlin to study the divine celestial movements.

The conclusion of the play also draws heavily upon the theme of a rightful king restored to his throne, the triumph of a true royal line over usurpers, and the prediction of the coming of King Arthur. The dangerous subjects of royal lineage and rights to thrones had presumably relaxed by the time this play was finally performed in the early to middle years of the seventeenth century.

### The Tempest and The Birth of Merlin

As William Shakespeare worked his way through certain of the chronicle histories and legends of Britain, creating new plays from historical and pseudo-historical characters and events, it seems strange that Arthur and Merlin did not feature in his list. Perhaps political events prevented him from attempting a play upon such potent mystical and nationalistic subjects. During the reign of Elizabeth it might have been possible, particularly in the atmosphere of 'Celtic' history researched by Dr John Dee. Dee defined a royal Celtic lineage whereby one Welsh prince Madoc sailed to the Americas, thereby assuring his distant heir Elizabeth of sovereignty over vast territories beyond the Atlantic (or as Dee called it: *Atlantean*) Ocean.

During the reign of James I, however, the subject of magic was extremely sensitive, as was the matter of royal lineage. Due to his most troubled and politically violent childhood, in which he was mainly under the dubious protection of highly political and powerful Scottish kirk elders, James developed a deep loathing of things magical. This was aggravated by charges laid against his mother, Mary Queen of Scots, that she practised witchcraft or other mysterious arts.

Thus a play about Merlin and rightful claiming of the British throne was not likely to guarantee royal approval when James became the first monarch of a yet-to-be united kingdom of England, Scotland, Wales and Ireland.

When Shakespeare wrote *Macbeth* he devised the character of Banquo to provide an originator for the Stuart dynasty and to emphasise their claim upon the throne. Banquo is not, in fact, a historical person, but a propagandist invention first appearing briefly in the chronicles of Hector Boecce, later in Holinshed, and finally developed by Shakespeare![4] The significance of Banquo in our present context is as an indicator of the politics that might have affected plays on the subject of kingship, so central to the legends of Merlin and Arthur.

But Merlin may indeed appear as Prospero in *The Tempest*, a comparison that has frequently been made, and must of course be the subject of detailed study in its own right. In this chapter there is only space to make some short comments upon *The Tempest*, its relationship to genuine Merlin lore, and its possible relationship, if any, to the *The Birth of Merlin*.

I mentioned above that it seems unlikely that Shakespeare had access to or could have read the *Vita Merlini*, and that the *Vita* does not seem to figure in *The Birth of Merlin*, though the *Prophecies* and the *History of the British Kings* certainly are major influences upon Rowley's plot. But we may find strong echoes of the *Vita* in *The Tempest*, too many to list in detail here, but enough to suggest that if Shakespeare wrote a 'Merlin' play, he applied his own magical creative ability to transform the British prophet into the magician of a new and perhaps less 'political' play than might have been written around Merlin himself.

To access the *Vita*, Shakespeare would have had to read Latin, and medieval Latin poetry in the artistic style of the twelfth century; this seems unlikely. But he might well have resorted to certain scholars and adepts, of whom Dr John Dee represents the epitome, who would almost certainly have studied the *Vita*; in any case, there are significant parallels. The following are the most obvious:

1. Both Merlin and Prospero grow beyond natural magic and abjure it, seeking instead to pursue a deeper spiritual enlightenment in which the magical forces and powers are left behind, realised at last to be merely super-sensual, or amplified energies of the natural world.

2. The central image and location is that of an Otherworld Island: in *The Tempest* it is ruled by the magician himself, while in the *Vita* it is ruled by one *Morgen*, mistress of magic, therapy and flight, to whom Merlin and the bard Taliesin take the mortally wounded Arthur for regeneration.

The Island of Apples which men call 'The Fortunate Isle' gets its name from the fact that it produces all things of itself; the fields there have no need of the ploughs of the farmer, and all cultivation is lacking except that which nature provides. Of its own accord it produces grain and grapes, and apple trees grow in its woods from the close-clipped grass. The ground of its own accord produces everything over and above mere grass, and people live there a hundred years or more.

Nine Sisters rule there by a pleasing set of laws those who come to them from our own country. She who is first of them is most skilled in the healing art, and excels her sisters in the beauty of her person. *Morgen* is her name, and she has learned what useful properties all the herbs contain, so that she can cure sick bodies. She also knows an art by which to change her shape, and to cleave the air on new wings like Daedalus; when she wishes she can be at Brest, Chartres, or Pavia, and when she wills, she slips down from the air onto your shores . . .

There after the battle of Camlann we took the wounded Arthur, guided by *Barinthus* to whom the waters and the stars of heaven were well known. With him steering the ship we arrived there with the king, Morgen receiving us with fitting honour, and in her chamber she placed the king upon a golden bed, and with her own hand she uncovered his honourable wound and gazed at it for a long time.

At length she said that health could be restored to him if he stayed with her for a long time and made use of her healing art. Rejoicing, therefore, we entrusted the king to her, and returning spread our sails to the favouring winds. [M.L.M.]

Modern interpreters of Shakespeare cite Dee's account of the Bermudas as a possible source for this island, yet it is well-rooted in British legend from pagan myths of the Otherworld, set across the sea to the west. British sources include Welsh legends such as the *Mabinogion*, Irish and Breton Lives of Saints, particularly the famous tales of St Brendan and his Navigation, and a large body of legend and poetry loosely related to Arthurian and Grail themes, in which magical islands play important roles.

Earlier sources, of course, are found in classical historians and geographers, and include the earliest known descriptions of Atlantis found in Plato's *Timaeus* and *Critias* and later the *Historical Library* of Diodorus Sicilus, writing during the reign of Julius Caesar. It was such mythology that, paradoxically to us cynical modern readers, encouraged John Dee to research and produce rigorously scientific maps and navigational aids for those Elizabethan gentleman adventurers who headed west seeking fortunes for themselves and dominions for their Virgin Queen.

3. An important character appears in the form of a Wild Man of the Woods: Caliban in the play, and, for a period, Merlin himself in the *Vita*. Both are representations of the Guardian or Lord of the Animals, or Wild Herdsman of Celtic mythology, firmly rooted in an ancient god of the wild, known from Romano-Celtic inscription (Paris, first century BC) as *Cernunnos*, 'the Horned One'.

This ancient image, conflated with that of the classical god Pan, was to appear in Renaissance Italy upon tarot cards as the Devil, possibly from *deo falsus* or false god, via the long historical, political and psychological route of the Roman Church through the Middle Ages. The Celtic god, The Hunter, Cernunnos, was remembered in oral tradition, in folk ceremonies involving dressing up as a stag (so firmly forbidden but St Augustine) and the common imagination, for many centuries after orthodox Christianity had become, apparently, firmly established. He appears, we should remember, as Herne the Hunter, who was said to reside mysteriously in Windsor Forest, and whose tradition was known also to William Shakespeare.

4. The balance, control and potency of the Four Elements are integral and essential to the operation of *The Tempest* and the *Vita*: and in both cases, the medieval and the Elizabethan, it is the cycle of, and ultimate liberation from, the Four Elements that enables and represents the true spiritual evolution of a central character.

None of the above matters seem to play any overt part in *The Birth of Merlin*, but they are present as undertones to the character and actions of the hairy little Merlin, so let us consider them afresh as they manifest in our play.

1. The precocious artichoke who reads deep books shortly after birth and makes a magical mockery of his clowning Uncle, suddenly becomes transformed into a very severe and spiritual character. He takes the side of the angels (literally) against the Devil, whom he imprisons in a rock. This is not identical to the more subtle transition shared by *The Tempest* and the *Vita*, for hairy Merlin continues to employ certain innate magical gifts, whereas the aged Merlin/Prospero abjures them altogether, even if it means losing apparent powers. But the undertone, of a higher order that replaces the initial precocious or abnormal powers, remains.

This is particularly interesting as a development of a higher order or role for Merlin, for the motif of his 'diabolical' father was emphasised in medieval sources, at a time when the orthodox Church sought to show Merlin as a type of Anti-Christ. Such propaganda was used by the Church to counter the enduring traditional popularity of Merlin in many parts of Wales, Brittany, Scotland, and (less certainly) Cornwall, England, Southern France, Northern Italy and Germany.

In fact, if we read Geoffrey of Monmouth's account of Merlin's parentage, we find that he is the child of a royal maiden and a *daemon* or Otherworld father. The *daemon* is not in any way related to the *demon* of orthodox propaganda, and is described clearly in Geoffrey's texts, especially the *Vita Merlini*, where classical cosmology is fused with a Celtic-Christian Otherworld vision and angelogy. In this schema, which may be, in part, traced back at least as far as the advisory spirit or *daemon* of Socrates, certain spirits mediate or travel between the Moon and Earth. Their role is to carry the prayers of humankind and the commands of divinity to one another, and they form the lower part of a harmonic sequence that includes angels and archangels (in a Christian symbolic sequence) or ancestral spirits and the Four Aeons or Great Powers of Being, in a pagan or Gnostic cosmology. In other words, they seem to represent a higher being or form of consciousness, yet are traditionally said to be close enough to humanity to interbreed. This is a very widespread and ancient theme indeed, with biblical sources from Hebrew tradition, classical equivalents in the dual parentage of certain heroes, and sacro-magical parallels in world religions, traditions, and folklore.

> When they [Merlin and his mother] were brought into his presence, King Vortigern received the mother with due courtesy, for he knew that she came of a noble family. Then he began to ask her by what man she had conceived the lad. 'By my living soul, Lord King,' she said, 'and by your living soul too, I did not have relations with any man to make me bear this child. I know only this; that, when I was in our private apartments with my sister nuns, some one used to come to me in the form of a most handsome young man. He would often hold me tightly in his arms and kiss me. When he had been some little time with me he would disappear, so that I could no longer see him. Many times too, when I was sitting alone, he would talk with me, without becoming visible, and when he came to see me in this way he would often make love with me, as a man would do, and in that way he made me pregnant. You must decide in your wisdom, my Lord, who was the father of this lad, for apart from what I have told, I have never had relations with a man'. (H.K.B.)

Maugantius was brought, and listened to her story, point by point. 'In the books written by our sages,' he said to Vortigern, 'and in many historical narratives, I have discovered that quite a number of men have been born in this way. As Apuleius asserts in the *De deo Socratis*, between the earth and the moon live spirits which we call incubus daemones. These have partly the nature of men and partly that of angels . . . it is possible that one of these appeared to this woman and begot the lad on her.' (H.K.B.)

This theme from classical sources was greatly developed in the cosmology set out by Geoffrey in his *Vita Merlini*, where the daemones are described as one part of a hierarchical or harmonic series of beings and forces, reaching from humanity to divinity.

In fact, the medieval attempt to make Merlin into an evil being failed, and he has never lost his place in literature first established by Nennius then developed by Geoffrey. By the time he appears in our seventeenth century comical play, his true nature reasserts itself, via the route of the essential goodness found in his human nature, through his love for his mother. This theme is balanced and reflected by the transformation of Joan in her beautiful last speech, in which the crude bawd becomes inspired and filled with poetic vision. And Stonehenge, of course, was built by Merlin as her memorial.

In most accounts, the stones are brought from Ireland to act as a memorial for Ambrosius, but in a curious manner the matriarchal dedication of *The Birth of Merlin* may be archaeologically more accurate, as we know that the megalithic culture of Britain and Ireland centred its religious impulse upon a Goddess of the Land, a variant of the Great Mother known throughout the ancient world.

2. The Otherworld Island does not appear in *The Birth of Merlin*. We have instead clear hints of a magical forest, and the locus of royal and prophetic power is clearly stated as the hill and tower wherein the young Merlin encounters King Vortigern. This motif is drawn direct from Geoffrey's preamble to the *Prophecies*, and was to appear in Renaissance tarot as the image of the Blasted Tower, which is found in folklore relating to certain ancient sites throughout Europe.

The Tower formed one essential unit in the old oral story-tellers' repertoire of such images, from which writers such as Geoffrey drew extensively, and into which tarot images were to return in later centuries as mnemonic aids. The most likely origin of visual cards for tarot may be the *Triumphs* of Petrarch, a set of poems developing traditional allegories, which were among the first to be

## The Birth of Merlin

illustrated with printed images, and contain many scenes similar to the first tarot cards hand-painted for Renaissance Princes.[5]

Both Geoffrey and Petrarch, in other words, though three centuries apart, drew upon an enduring bardic or story-tellers' tradition that contained key images nowadays found in tarot, but originally deriving from pagan myth and religion.

The image and scene of the Blasted Tower and its underlying cavern, is also the source for an important vision of Two Dragons. In the *History* they arise from a pool beneath Vortigern's tower, and their ensuing battle not only symbolises the struggle between Celts and Saxons, but triggers off Merlin's remarkable and chaotic *Prophecies* which reach to the end of the Solar System, dealing almost exclusively with British history and future history.

The Dragons are also found in the Welsh Celtic legend of Lludd and Llevelys, in which a king imprisons them in a vessel or chest at a location in the centre of the land; he does so to maintain stability and peace.

'And the second plague' [said Llevelys to his brother Lludd] 'that is in thy dominion, behold it is dragon. And another dragon of a foreign race is fighting with it, and striving to overcome it. And therefore does this dragon make a fearful outcry. And in this wise mayest thou come to know the truth of this. After thou hast returned home, cause the island [of Britain] to be measured in its length and breadth, and in the place where is the exact central point, there cause a pit to be dug, and cause a cauldron full of the best mead that can be brewed to be put in the pit, with a covering of satin over the face of the cauldron. And then, in thine own person, do thou remain there watching, and thou will see the dragons fighting in the form of terrifying animals. And at length they will take the form of dragons in the air. And last of all they will fall in the form of two pigs upon the satin covering, and they will sink in, and the covering with them, and they will draw it down to the very bottom of the cauldron. And they will drink up the whole of the mead, and after that they will fall asleep. Thereupon do you immediately fold the covering around them, and bury them in a kist [chest] in the strongest place that thou hast in thy dominions, and hide them deep within the earth. And as long as they shall bide in that strong place, no plague shall come to the Island of Britain from elsewhere.' [From *Lludd and Llevelys* (*The Mabinogion*), translated by Lady Charlotte Guest.]

## The Childe hath found his Father

Curiously, this legend reads like the first half of the tale, with Vortigern, the usurper or false king, later acting as the cause of an illicit or even sacrilegious release of those same dragons originally imprisoned by a rightful king. In terms of literary history, however, Geoffrey's account of Vortigern precedes the story of Lludd and Llevelys in the *Mabinogion* by three centuries or more; yet tradition is not bounded by historical time, and both themes are drawn from a Celtic tradition concerning the role of kingship and the sanctity of the land.[6]

[The youthful Merlin has revealed that an underground chamber containing a pool is the cause of collapse of King Vortigern's Tower . . .] Then said he to the king 'command the pool to be drained, and at the bottom you will see two hollow stones, and in them two dragons asleep.' The king did not hesitate to believe him, since he had found true what Merlin had said of the pool, and therefore ordered it to be drained. Which done, he found all as Merlin had said, and was possessed of the greatest admiration of him.

And while Vortigern, King of the Britons, was seated upon the bank of the pool that had been drained, there issued forth two dragons, whereof one was white and the other red. And when they drew close to one another, they grappled together in terrible combat, and breathed forth fire. But presently the White Dragon prevailed, and drove the Red to the verge of the pool. But he, grieving to be thus driven, fell fiercely upon the White and forced him to draw back. And whilst they were fighting in this wise, the King bade Ambrosius Merlin declare what this battle of the Dragons portended. [P.V.M.]

3. The Wild Man of both *The Tempest* and the *Vita Merlini* is, to a certain extent, the weird and hairy Merlin himself, an adult infant. Furthermore it is likely that the visual image of his father, the Devil, is drawn from this same tradition, found in folk ritual drama . . . his head is *horrid*, (page 48) which is to say shaggy or hairy. But by nature the Devil in *The Birth of Merlin* is unquestionably the suave evil potentate of repressed Christian imagination, he who had long since come to the aid of a tyrannical Church and state. He is not the ancient, and, incidentally, *beneficial* being deriving from the pagan Celtic god Cernunnos, who originally kept herds healthy and drew wealth from the secret earth for the benefit of those who understood his strict laws.

## Familiarity of the Traditional Themes and Legends in *The Birth of Merlin* to the Sixteenth- and Seventeenth-Century Audience

If we consider the legendary and magical elements within *The Birth of Merlin*, they present a curious and paradoxical mixture. Merlin, for example, is a hairy man-child, a comical apparition, given to magic and prophecy, yet he ultimately defeats the forces of darkness, and imprisons the Devil, who, incidentally, had been found to be his father. He also, in a delightful departure from an older tradition preserved by medieval chroniclers concerning Merlin, builds Stonehenge as a tribute to his mother, the lascivious Joan Go-too't. So is he a good character, or a bad one? Is he the semi-divine prophetic child of legend, or the Devil-born spawn of Hell as in medieval propaganda? Somehow the playwrights, Rowley and A. N. Other have fused both images of Merlin into one character, a person who begins as a silly little artichoke but leaves us in no doubt as to his full power by the conclusion of the play.

One most intriguing question concerns the audience of the day; how familiar were they with the magical, traditional, and mythic aspects of the play? This is an important and unavoidable question, for many of the matters within the text are obscure, and some might have been areas of high risk for the writer and performer, were it not for the highly skilled fusion of religion and humour, forbidden arts and bawdry. Furthermore, the concept of a hilarious comedy wedded to Celtic legendary history and mythology may be bizarre to the modern reader, but it seems to have presented no problem to the audience of the late sixteenth or early seventeenth century.

Indeed, the great success of the play today is still its successful fusion of mirth and magic, while a further theme, that of spirituality and chastity is perhaps uncomfortable or even obscure for our time and culture. The mixture is very rich, and it cannot have been played to an audience unfamiliar with its constituent elements, especially as it starred a popular writer and performer, 'beloved by Shakespeare, Fletcher and Jonson', leading comedian in the Prince of Wales' Men (1613).

One of the keys to the magical elements of *The Birth of Merlin* is found in the simple yet important fact that it was written as vehicle for William Rowley; we may reduce this further and say that one of the secrets of the success of the play is that it is based upon a Clown. The theatrical role of Clown is dealt with in the chapter by Roy Hudd, but in the context of magic and legend we must look at the Clown or Fool in tradition, esoteric or magical arts, and most significantly in folklore.

It is in British folk tradition that we may find the roots of this play, and the grand legendary-historic themes and events of the plot, such as the invasion of the Saxons, the treachery of Vortigern, and the announcement of the once and future king Arthur, are in truth scenery upon which the perennial Fool capers, accompanied by his bawdy sister and magical nephew.

We might remember, at this point in the discussion, that the relationship between a man and his sister's son, uncle and nephew, was at one time of great importance in Celtic culture, and in ancient times was held to be a greater bond than that of fatherhood. This tradition, which derives perhaps from a very early matriarchal or matrilinear social structure, persists in a number of obscure but recognisable ways within folk tradition and early poetry, song, literature, and drama. Thus the Clown, Merlin and Joan, are not merely witty inventions to dress up an old subject, they are primal figures with an enduring history, generating, perhaps, an unconscious recognition.

Like many primal figures, including those of certain gods and goddesses, they are figures of ridicule behaving absurdly, yet each is found to have a distinct and redeeming power of his or her own. This theme of grotesque comedy fused inseparably with great creative or regenerative power, is found in myths from both Celtic and classical Greek cultures, and has many parallels worldwide.

In the context of tradition, folklore, and popular collective entertainment, there can be no doubt that the English London audience would have been on familiar ground: street entertainments; festivals, social entertainments and family parties, all drew heavily upon a well-established oral tradition. How much of this familiarity applies to Merlin, Vortigern, and Aurelius, who are the stuff of Welsh legendary history, is another complex matter. It must be sufficient, for the moment, to state that with one or two rare exceptions, Arthurian and Merlin legends play no part whatsoever in English folk tradition.

Before outrage is cried, and if anyone doubts my assertion, for there is a popular fallacy that Arthurian legends are ingrained upon English folk tradition, let the doubter consult the reference collections of English folklore, tales, and songs, found in any major library. Arthur and his knights are conspicuously absent from English oral lore, despite (rather than because of) their vast presence in literature.

Before considering the themes and characters from tradition in *The Birth of Merlin* and their connection to the legends of Merlin, we should first briefly consider the nature of oral or folk traditions. At the time of the play's writing there was a flourishing body of anonymous music, song, poetry, dance and drama, deriving from a collective oral tradition. This simply means that people learned it from one another, drawing material from a large repertoire held in common, a national repertoire which, as modern folklorists and anthropologists tell us, has international parallels. I do not intend to venture upon an academic analysis of the Shakespearian claims of *The Birth of Merlin*, being unqualified to do so, but a few comparisons and suggestions may be valid in the context of this chapter on the magical themes, symbols, and traditions in the play.

Many of the themes in *The Birth of Merlin* which might seem to suggest the work of Shakespeare, who frequently drew upon folkloric themes and motifs such as abound in this play, are typical of the exchange from oral tradition to formalised text, an exchange which occurs repeatedly in literature from the medieval period to the present day. Much of the historical matter in our play comes from the work of Geoffrey of Monmouth (albeit at several removes), who was the first British writer take extensive oral tradition and render it into a master work of literature. This was, of course, his *History of the British Kings*, containing the separate book of *The Prophecies of Merlin* written out into Latin during the middle years of the twelfth century. As we know, many of the Shakespeare's historical or legendary sources were drawn from Holinshed's *Chronicles*, which in turn were taken from those of Geoffrey and other earlier writers.

The *Prophecies* and a passage in the *History* immediately preceding them, in which the youthful Merlin confronts Vortigern and his corrupt magicians, are major sources for the plot of our play. Geoffrey also wrote, a few years later, a sophisticated, highly skilled, and profound *Life of Merlin* in elegant Latin verse, though this does not seem, at first, to play much part in our play. I say 'at first', because there is a very strong and pertinent link between the seventeenth-century play and the rare *Vita Merlini* which our playwrights almost certainly could not have read or consulted, a link that may be traced back to pagan Celtic religion, and to a small number of ancient Scottish and Irish literary renderings of Celtic oral tradition. This link is found in the character of Clown or Fool.

For the present, however, we must pursue our trail of folklore in the seventeenth century, and its presence and familiarity among the audience of the day, the people to whom *The Birth of Merlin* was, presumably, 'acted to great applause' by William Rowley and his skilled company.

As everyone knows, or ought to know, the English Revolution disposed of royalty and decapitated Charles I in 1649. The Puritans also banned certain popular ceremonies as being too pagan and lascivious in nature for god-fearing English men and women to indulge in. It is to these ceremonies, often connected to ancient seasonal festivals, that we may trace, in part, the characters in *The Birth of Merlin*. Such seasonal festivals were the remnants of fertility religion and its cycle of the seasons linked in the remote past, through sacrifice, to the health of the land and its people. Many enduring folk ceremonies such as May Day are echoes of this type of essentially pagan religion, no matter what Christian dressing they may occasionally wear.

In country regions during the sixteenth and seventeenth centuries, local rituals and customs abounded; in the city such ancient customs were also preserved, though they tended to have more of a spectacular or entertainment value than a fundamental relationship to the cycle of the seasons. Folk rituals, such as Mummers' Plays, were part of the popular customs and entertainment of Rowley's audience, and we only need to examine the types of character that appear to find their connections to *The Birth of Merlin*. A Fool, a lascivious man-woman often with a fatherless child, a wise-man or doctor, and the devil, are the central characters in these age-old rituals.

In many examples, the Fool or another central hero, is killed and revived with much lewdity and nonsense. In some specific ceremonies, we find this resurrection theme linked to other ritual displays: rapper-sword dancing in the North of England, where a man is apparently decapitated only to revive, or various hobby-horse dances in which the horse dies and is brought back to life. Such ceremonies are connected to the great festival of May, the turning-point of the pagan year, and were vitally important to those old English festivities that were eventually banned by the Puritans of the short-lived Commonwealth.

The reader will notice that there are connections to the characters in *The Birth of Merlin* and also to the sacrificial themes found in The *Vita Merlini* and other early sources drawing from pagan tradition. The man dressed up as a woman, for example, is a deliberately ambiguous role that is known from ancient classical sources; we find this defined in the context of the Threefold Death in the *Vita Merlini*, while the Threefold Death itself was originally a myth of sacrifice and resurrection.

The Fool of the Mummers' Play is our Clown, while the Doctor or Wise Man (who resurrects the dead Fool with spells and vile medicine) is, in a positive aspect, Anselm the Hermit, or in a negative aspect, Proximus. The Devil is, of course, himself. The grotesque man/woman of folk ritual, usually the largest most virile male available but dressed as a female, becomes Joan Go-too't, though we have noted from other traditions that there may also be a further link between this hermaphrodite character and the Fool. It would be of particular interest to know if Joan was played by a man or a woman in Rowley's company, as women were beginning to appear on the stage at approximately the time of our play. This would further clarify the connection of Joan to a 'modern' character known to us all, and certainly drawn from folk ritual, the man/woman Dame of the Pantomime.

## Bibliography

(A short list; the books suggested deal in depth with many of the subjects touched upon in this chapter, and also contain extensive lists of sources, cross references, and related publications for further reading.)

1a: *John Dee*, Charlotte Fell Smith, Constable & Co, London, 1909.
 b: *The Heptarchia Mystica of John Dee* (ed. Robert Turner) Number 17, Magnum Opus Hermetic Sourceworks Series, Edinburgh, 1983.
 c: 'John Dee, The Elizabethan Merlin', Gareth Knight in *Merlin and Woman (The Book of the Second Merlin Conference)* ed. R. J. Stewart, Blandford Press, London, 1988.
2a: *Celtic Gods and Goddesses*, R. J. Stewart (illustrated Miranda Gray) Blandford Press London, 1989.
 b: *Where is Saint George? (Pagan Imagery in English Folksong)*, R. J. Stewart, Blandford Press, London, 1988.
3a: *Mabon and the Mysteries of Britain*, Caitlin Matthews, Penguin Arkana, London, 1987.
 b: 'Merlin in the Earliest Records', Geoffrey Ashe in *The Book of Merlin (The First Merlin Conference)*, ed. R. J. Stewart, Blandford Press, Poole, 1987, paperback 1988.
 c: *The Mystic Life of Merlin*, R. J. Stewart, Penguin Arkana, London, 1986.
4: *Macbeth, Scotland's Warrior King*, R. J. Stewart, Firebird Books, Poole, 1988.
5: *The Merlin Tarot*, R. J. Stewart, book and deck of cards, painted and illustrated by Miranda Gray, Aquarian Press, Wellingborough, 1988.
6a: *Celtic Heritage*, Alwyn and Brinley Rees, Thames & Hudson, London, 1961.
 b: *Pagan Celtic Britain*, Anne Ross, Cardinal, London, 1974.

# THESE ARE THE QUESTIONS TO ASK:
# Who? When? Why? Where? How?
## *Denise Coffey*

**Who?**

Of Merlin and his skill what region doth not hear?
The World shall still be full of Merlin everywhere.
A thousand lingering years his prophecies have run,
And scarcely shall have end till time itself be done.

These lines from Michael Drayton's *Poly-Olbion* (1612) have their echo in *The Birth of Merlin* (1623?) (1620?) . . .

All future times shall still record this story,
Of Merlin's learned worth and Arthur's glory.

And Merlin's name in Brittain shall live,
Whilst men inhabit here, or Fates can give
Power to amazing wonder, envy shall weep,
And mischief sit and shake her ebbone wings,
Whilst all the world of Merlin's magic sings.

In these days the oaks shall burn in the forest glades and acorns shall burgeon on the lime trees' boughs.

The Severn Sea shall flow through seven mouths and the River Usk shall be boiling hot for seven months. Its fish die because of the heat and from them serpents will be born. . .

The baths shall grow cold at Bath and its health-giving waters shall breed death.

London shall mourn the death of twenty thousand and the Thames will be turned into blood. . .

. . . the Moon's chariot shall run amok in the Zodiac and the Pleaides will burst into tears. . . In the twinkling of an eye the seas shall rise up and the arena of the winds shall be opened once again.

The winds shall do battle together with a blast of ill-omen, making their din reverberate from one constellation to another. [From the Prophecies of Merlin in Geoffrey of Monmouths' twelfth-century

*History of the Kings of Britain*, translated by Lewis Thorpe, Penguin Classics]
At that time shall the stones speak, and the area towards the Gallic coast be contracted into a narrow space. On each bank shall one man hear another, and the soil of the island shall be enlarged. The secrets of the deep shall be revealed, and Gaul shall tremble with fear. [R. J. Stewart, *The Prophetic Vision of Merlin*, Arkana, 1986]

Could this refer to the Channel Tunnel? Bob Stewart is the Merlin specialist, so turn at once to his chapter to read more on the subject.

Merlin seems never to have been entirely absent from our consciousness from the first emerging of the legend of the mighty seer; in every century there have been representations, added stories, images, all to the taste and fashion of the generation that rediscovers him. From esoteric paintings, to Disney cartoon, to souvenir tea-towels, Merlin is everywhere as everything.

I was sitting quietly at home when Merlin intruded into my life via a speaking stone (as prophesied: 'in that time the stones shall speak') or telephone, as we call it. Bob Stewart (R. J. Stewart, as above) asked me to read a play which had been brought to his attention. I was interested at once by the names on the front page; hadn't I heard them somewhere . . . 'written by William Shakespeare and William Rowley'. The text was that of the Tudor Facsimile, published in 1910 in reproduction of the original seventeenth-century print and punctuation.

Imagine how my heart was thudding. Could there be a Shakespeare-attributed play neglected and unplayed for hundreds of years? It would be like finding a piece previously unknown, by Mozart, in the attic among the sheet music between a faded copy of 'Red Sails in the Sunset' and *The Daily Express Christmas Singalong Book*.

The text off the play arrived, trailing mystery with it.

## When?

Date of writing not known – about 1620–1623. Wait a minute! When did Shakespeare die? 23 April 1616. Ah! So what's his name doing on the title page of the only known edition of the play, published in 1662? The director turns detective. What does the *Dictionary of National Biography* have to say on the matter? 'A bookseller's fib', that's what it says. So Francis Kirkman and Henry Marsh were selling the play at the Princes Arms in Chancery Lane in 1662 under false pretences as being written by William Shakespeare and

William Rowley; and what about the other claim on the front page? 'as it hath been several times acted with great applause'? That sounds more likely – why would they want to publish a play that hadn't been popular? Or were Messrs Kirkman and Marsh publishers of more fiction in their advertisements than in their works? Their stated wish on the front page is *'Placere cupio'* . . . 'I hope to please'. I did what any detective would do. I read the evidence carefully. Rather, that's what I meant to do, but the play whirled me along in its robust, vigorous, funny, dramatic, magical style, and read as lively and fresh as a new musical or a very classy pantomime.

The character of the Clown particularly interested me. This must have been played by William Rowley himself; was he rotund? When he and his extremely pregnant sister are asked 'How now, what are you?' the Clown replies 'A couple of Great Brittains, you may see by our bellies, sir.' William Rowley, always second billing, collaborator with many of the best-known and successful playwrights of the time, known as an amiable man and a dependable collaborator, with a good line in jokes and a turn for pathos. I wonder who the part of the sister, Joan Go-too't was written for? The Clown and his sister are searching for the gentleman with 'most rich attire, a fair hat and feather, a gilt sword, and most excellent hangers' who has accosted and seduced Joan in the wood, hence her pregnant state. The characters of brother and sister are clearly written for a comic duo, used to working with each other, and, I would imagine, popular favourites. Will Rowley was an actor in the Prince of Wales Company (Charles, later Charles I), and if the meagre information about him is accurate, he was a great friend of Shakespeare's, among other writers and actors. London was then a relatively small town, with a limited circle of actors, so suppose we look at the mystery from another starting-point? 'Supposes' is a perfectly good Elizabethan game; let's play.

Suppose Will Shakespeare is in process of writing *King Lear* . . . the likely source of the original story is to be found in Geoffrey of Monmouth's *Historia Regum Britanniae*, completed in 1136; Geoffrey's source for this overview of the history of the kings of Britain was 'a certain very ancient book, written in the British language'. One of the pre-Roman kings was King Leir, who had three daughters named Goneril, Regan, Cordelia . . . As was Shakespeare's wont and genius, he took the bones of the legend or historical fact depending upon your academic opinion, and fashion from it his great play *King Lear*. Or, rather two versions, the second a revised script which includes a speech by the Fool which is a comic prophesying in the style of . . . well, here it is –

## Act Three, Scene Three

[Exeunt LEAR and KENT]

FOOL: This is a brave night to cool a courtezan.
 I'll speak a prophecy ere I go:
 When priests are more in word than matter;
 When brewers mar their malt with water;
 When nobles are their tailor's tutors;
 No heretics burned but wenches' suitors;
 When every case in law is right;
 No squire in debt, nor no poor knight;
 When slanders do not live in tongues;
 Nor cutpurses come not to throngs;
 When usurers tell their gold i' the field;
 And bawds and whores do churches build;
 Then shall the realm of Albion
 Come to great confusion;
 Then comes the time, who lives to see'it
 That going shall be us'd with feet.
 This prophecy Merlin shall make; for I live before his time.

Why did mention of Merlin turn up in the revision? Was the speech a parody of Poly-Olbion style? Or an actor's addition? Or in response to some topical situation? Or . . . or, suppose that the two Wills, Shakespeare and Rowley, had a conversation in which Geoffrey of Monmouth's works were discussed as a fruitful field for plots for plays. (Cymbeline was another King in the *History*.) The book would still have been only available in Latin at that time, probably the 1587 edition, and did Rowley read Latin? The argument as to whether Shakespeare did or didn't read Latin is a long-running academic entertainment; I assume he did. Suppose the story of Merlin was discussed in the way stories often are, starting with the bare bones of a plot, thinking of characters, odd scraps of scenes, odd lines, jokes, supposes. Suppose Merlin in Shakespeare's mind. Did he add the Fool's soliloquy, containing a few recognisable themes: for example the remark – 'When every case in Law is right' sounds possible from that well-known Litigator, Mr W.S.? The Fool foretells the coming of Merlin, so becomes a greater seer than the great man himself! As far as I can tell from a swift glance at the Shakespeare concordance, there is only one other mention of Merlin in all the plays: a passing reference to 'the dreamer Merlin' in early years in a Henry History. With the revived public interest in all things Ancient, Magical and British, Merlin as a character seems a logical progression from the other British legendary themes for Shakespeare to explore; and I believe he did, but in his own inimitable way, in *The Tempest*.

Suppose he and Rowley had started the kind of collaboration I've described above, meeting for conversations, suggestions, scraps of structure, a drink, some jokes, good company, but the play no further advanced, sticking, perhaps on Shakespeare's point that the theme should not be merely a retelling of the legend, displaying the effects of magical powers, but an exploration of the human aspects of such power. How do you use extraordinary powers? What is your responsibility if you possess such power? ('They that have power to hurt, and will do none' – Sonnet 94.) Prospero is the mighty magician in *The Tempest*, but resolves the play by the qualities of reason, Christian forgiveness, and casting aside dependence on magical powers and progressing to a state of human potential to improve, progress, enrich, without recourse to superstition or outside magical forces. Was this Shakespeare's Merlin play? Prospero, the rightful Duke of Milan (pronounced M*i*lan, not Mi*lan* as now; M*i*lan sounds not unlike M*er*lin . . . W.S. was partial to puns . . .) when told by Ariel, the airy spirit, of the tearful, penitent state of those who had wronged him, and are held prisoner by his magic power, reacts thus:

> Though with their high wrongs I am struck to the quick
> Yet, with my nobler reason, 'gainst my fury
> Do I take part: the rarer action is
> In virtue than in vengeance: they being penitent,
> The sole drift of my purpose doth extend
> Not a frown further. Go, release them, Ariel.
> My charms I'll break, their senses I'll restore,
> And they shall be themselves.

ARIEL: I'll fetch them, sir.                              [Exit]

PROSPERO: Ye elves of hills, brooks, standing lakes, and groves;
> And ye, that on the sands with printless foot
> Do chase the ebbing Neptune, and do fly him
> When he comes back; you demy puppets that
> By moonshine do the green-sour ringlets make,
> Whereof the ewe not bites; and you, whose pastime
> Is to make midnight mushrooms; that rejoice
> To hear the solemn curfew; by whose aid
> (Weak masters though ye be) I have bedimm'd
> The noontide sun, called forth the mutinous winds,
> And twixt the green sea and the azur'd vault
> Set roaring war; to the dread rattling thunder

> Have I given fire, and rifted Jove's stout oak
> With his own bolt: the strong bas'd promontory
> Have I made shake; and by the spurs pluck'd up
> The pine and cedar: graves, at my command,
> Have wak'd their sleepers; oped, and let them forth
> By my so potent art. But this rough magic
> I here abjure; and, when I have required
> Some heavenly music, (which even now I do)
> To work mine end upon their senses, that
> This airy charm is for, I'll break my staff,
> Bury it certain fathoms in the earth,
> And deeper than did ever plummet sound,
> I'll drown my book.                    [Solemn Music]

This 'rough magic' is akin to the magic of Oberon and Puck, a countryman's magic, in which the behaviour of the elements and of natural circumstances was given fantastic explanations, far more potent and thrilling than any scientific revelation of later centuries. What is the knowledge that tides are governed by the moon compared to Shakespeare's nameless ones that on the sands with printless foot do chase the ebbing Neptune, and do fly him when he comes back? There's certainly no hint of writing of the quality of Shakespeare in *The Birth of Merlin*, although two pieces of evidence (which I can only defend from an instinctive feeling) suggest that Shakespeare influenced the making of the play. The first example is one of the four strands of plot which weave their way through the play. This fourfold plot is one of the sources of vitality in the play, giving it great energy, with many different facets; but in practical terms it's expensive for a modern theatre, because it needs so many actors. Some of the editing I'll do for production will be for practical, not artistic reasons. The four strands of plot are:

1. The 'King Lear in reverse' plot. Donobert, an old nobleman, has two daughters, Modestia and Constantia. They are wooed, and, at first it seems, won, by young Cador Earl of Cornwall, and Edwyn, son of the Earl of Gloster. The course of their betrothal takes an unusual turn, however.
2. The Clown and his sister plot. The search for the putative father of the soon-to-be-born-child. Searching through wood and Court.
3. The King and the Saxon Princess plot. In which King Aurelius is enchanted, and his brother falls prey to the same spell, with destructive results.

4. Merlin's impact on the world, from the moment of miraculous birth to the vision of the future of Brittain's royal lineage and history.

These are very terse descriptions of the story lines, but as they interweave, the play proceeds to a rich mixture of magic, mystery, battles, and breezy comedy, with moments of true pathos and frightening danger, music and (with a big cast of actors) spectacle.

In plot 1, which is, as far as I know, a very original idea, there is a speech given to Modestia, so musical in its construction that we may make it a song in the production. (Please, by the way, remember that what you read here may *not* be what happens in the finished production, which will be composed of everybody's inspiration and work.) Anyway, this speech of Modestia is affectingly simple:

MODESTIA: . . . oh, my good sister, hear me,
   This world is but a Masque, catching weak eyes,
   With what is not our selves but our disguise,
   A Vizard that falls off, the Dance being done,
   And leaves Death's Glass for all to look upon,
   Our best happiness here, lasts but a night,
   Whose burning Tapers makes false Ware seem right;
   Who knows not this, and will not now provide
   Some better shift before his shame be spy'd,
   And knowing this vain world at last shall leave him,
   Shake off these robes that help but to deceive him.

Not Shakespeare by any reckoning, but Shakespeare-influenced?

Suppose the Wills were discussing the strand of the play of which Modestia is part. The unusual idea in the scene is that a wedding procession is stopped by the sister of the bride, who has become so influenced by the Hermit that she has renounced the world. She in her turn influences the bride so that she too gets her to a nunnery. Could this perhaps have been suggested by the man who created the darkly comic-tragic wedding scene in *Much Ado About Nothing*?

The other moment in the play where I feel a Shakespearian influence is the transformation of Joan Go-too't after the birth of Merlin. King Vortigern, speaking of the astonishing child/man that is Merlin, asks 'What was his father?' Joan, abashed at being in such a presence as the King's is lost for words. Merlin gently tells her:

     Mother speak freely and unastonisht,
     That which you dar'd to act, dread not to name.

And Joan, under the influence of her remarkable son, speaks in a style completely unlike her way of speaking previously, which has matched the Clown's vigorous style of cheerful bawdry.

JOAN: In pride of blood and beauty did I live, my glass the Altar was, my face the Idol, such was my peevish love unto my self, that I did hate all other, such disdain was in my scornful eye, that I supposed no mortal creature worthy to enjoy me, thus with the Peacock I beheld my train, but never saw the blackness of my feet, oft have I chid the winds for breathing on me, and curst the Sun, fearing to blast my beauty, in midst of his most leaprous disease, a seeming fair young man appear'd unto me, in all things suiting my aspiring pride, and with him brought along a conquering power, to which my frailty yielded, from whose embrace this issue came, what more he is, I know not.

Not written by W.S., but there's an echo there . . .

HAMLET: . . . so loving to my mother
That he might not beteem the winds of Heaven
Visit her face too roughly . . .

Joan Go-too't chides the winds for breathing on her. Yes, it's a frail connection, and there's no reason why Rowley wasn't perfectly capable of writing in different styles – as a collaborator with other writers, he'd be used to that – but maybe this section is a clue to the identity of the co-writer, if there was one, of *The Birth of Merlin*.

William Rowley's dates of birth and death are surrounded by query marks in every work of reference I've seen. 1585?–1642? Apparently there were other Rowleys in the theatre with whom he is often confused. Poor William Rowley, second billing again. The *Dictionary of National Biography* informs us that Will retired as an actor in 1627, having been a leading comedian in many companies, 'beloved of Shakespeare, Fletcher, Jonson'. Best-known for his collaborations with Thomas Middleton, most notably *The Changeling* (and at the time of writing there is a production of this play running at the National Theatre). His verse, according to the same source, has 'a metrical harshness and irregularity'. He is praised, however, for his rare vein of whimsical humour and unexpected mastery of tragic pathos.

So, round about 1620–23, he would have been 35 or 38, well into middle age. Shakespeare would have been dead for at least four years, having retired from the theatre and left London years before. The reason for this is not known, but here's my suppose . . .

There seems to have been a resurgence of interest in things anciently British, and in chivalry, with jousting at the Barricades as a grand spectator event, and plays with masques, music, dancing and spectacle. Had Shakespeare, with his word music and insight into the human condition, become unfashionable? For whatever reason, he left for Stratford. Suppose then, that four years after Shakespeare's death, Will Rowley remembers, or finds notes, or feels the time is ripe for, the Merlin project begun but abandoned years before. When he prepared the script, he would want to acknowledge his friend's contribution by a credit on the frontispiece, even though Shakespeare had not written text. And William Rowley (always second billing) would put his more distinguished colleague's name first. I consulted Professor Harold H. Brooks M.A D. Litt. (Oxon) Honorary Fellow St Edmund's Hall, Oxford, and a distinguished Editor of the Arden Shakespeare series. What did he think of my 'Rowley-attributing' suppose? He generously took time to consider it and replied: 'If there *is* a genuine Shakespeare connection with *The Birth of Merlin*, your hypothesis suggests about the only way it could reasonably have happened.' But when he read the play this was his verdict:

> I see nothing in it that Shakespeare is likely to have suggested. This seems to me nothing but another item in the Shakespeare Apocrypha, and not one of the less implausible. So if it is worth editing and producing – as it may be – it must be for its own sake, not bolstered by any Shakespearean interest. We do not know that the Shakespeare claim goes back to 1620; it may be no more than the booksellers' ploy in 1662. Shakespeare's name at that time would be a selling point: the Elizabethan dramatists held in great esteem immediately after the Restoration were Fletcher, Jonson and Shakespeare.

Professor Brooks had many more words of wisdom for me, and was most generously helpful in suggesting other sources of scholarly opinion about the play and the meagre information on its history.

But it was time to leave Supposes and face facts. Goodbye groves of Academe, hello market-place.

## Why?

Is *The Birth of Merlin* worth a production? Is it worth the fiendishly difficult process of getting a budget together, and worth the actor's energies? Would an audience in the late twentieth century enjoy the play? We had the text typed in clear form. I read it again. The play's vitality and variety, its energy and good humour and brisk adventure, together with the magic sequences and the flashes of originality, beguiled me again.

The play is clearly written by an actor for actors to play at full blast, and for an audience to relish. There are no deeply obscure seventeenth-century jokes or incomprehensible puns for poor sweating twentieth-century actors to play, with whatever comic embellishment they can muster, to a soap-opera-sated audience. There are, however, elements of the best of what has become pantomime tradition – devil, apparitions, handsome princes, wicked princess, a good magician and an evil magician in a battle of spells, battles, transformation scenes, comic characters in dangerous adventures, music, dancing, fights, spectacle; book now for Christmas!

### Where?

Where should Merlin re-emerge? Iain McIntosh, of Theatre Projects, when told of the Merlin play, suggested the theatr at Clwyd. Not only was it fitting for Merlin to reappear in Wales, but it's the kind of play which might very well interest Toby Robertson, Artistic Director of Clwyd. Bob Stewart and I went to see his splendid production of *Edward III*, another Shakespeare Apocryphal play, but with a stronger claim to pedigree than *The Birth of Merlin*. Toby was enthusiastic about the project, and, at the time of writing this chapter, it seems as if there may very well be a production at Theatr Clwyd next year. But big productions of this kind are very complex to arrange, financially, practically; and, most important of all, in getting the casting right. As usual, Time will Tell.

### How?

I read the play several times. The text would benefit from pruning, and, in the case of the penultimate scene of the play, rearranging the sequence of the Donobert/Gloster scene so that it forms an epilogue, instead of stopping the grand sweep of the play towards its end. If an epilogue, why not prologue? What about a joust across Time's barriers? Suppose the audience starts its outing in our own time, at an entertainment. A club comic launches into his act, dressed in the height of clubland fashion. His brisk and risqué jokes titillate the audience and tickle their collective fancy.

Suddenly his voice is not his own; instead of the tag of the joke about his wife being so mean, so mean, so mean, she bought a black and white dog because she thought the licence was cheaper . . . he says, in the voice of Merlin:

> All future times shall record the story
> Of Merlin's learned worth and Arthur's glory.

Recovering from his momentary lapse, he tries to battle on with some jokes about Wales, and is again wiped out, Merlin's voice, even stronger, taking over:

> Report the wonders of his name and glory
> While there are tongues and times to tell his story . . .

This with lighting effects to change the stage from a brash, modern, club Sunday night concert atmosphere to the mysterious depths of fifth-century Brittain, sound and music to influence and affect us as Merlin invades our time and space.

The comedian struggles for a final regaining of his own personality and time, but his strength is gone, and Merlin's voice speaks in triumphant timbre:

> And Merlin's name in Brittain shall live,
> Whilst Men inhabit here, or Fates can give
> Power to amazing wonder, envy shall weep,
> And mischief sit and shake her ebbone wings,
> Whilst all the World of Merlin's magic sings.

Suddenly people from the fifth century are on the stage in mid-conversation, ignoring the comedian, who finds he has become invisible. Donobert and Gloster, Modestia and Constantia, Edwin and Cador play the first scene of Actus I. We are in the Court of King Aurelius, the play has begun, with the audience drawn into the same time-intrusion as the comedian has been. At the end of the first scene, the comedian is beckoned from a corner, by an unseen woman, calling to him, 'Brother! Here!'. The comedian warily goes towards the unseen speaker, and the beckoning hand. One hand becomes two, strong, grabbing, and the comedian is hauled off, protesting, into darkness. Meanwhile, the second scene is in progress. So the play would proceed, one scene nearly overlapping the next, cutting like film; faces lit in solo fine spotlights, so that we see the characters in close-up; the stage begins to be visible as the play proceeds, growing to the full spectacle of the aerial battle between the red dragon and the white, the Devil being imprisoned in a rock, the weaving dance of the Fates attending the birth of Merlin, the battles, the wedding processions, the apparitions conjured by Merlin showing the future of Brittain's royal lineage.

How should the play be performed? In what style? And within what economic restrictions? There's no point, in my opinion, in doing a 'museum theatre' production: trying to recreate as closely as possible the original style of the Jacobean, and possibly Restoration, performances wouldn't work unless the audience knew that what they were to see was a recreation of a past style; theatre is a transitory, living art, and every generation interprets within its, and its audience's, own experience. A 'museum' performance is a curiosity, not a true theatrical event. With unlimited budget it would certainly be interesting to try to recreate an Inigo Jones style spectacle, but our first production will be modestly funded.

It's clear from the text that Will Rowley conceived of his characters as wearing the clothes of his own time (the feathered hat and gilt sword of the mysterious gentleman in the woods describe a seventeenth-century gent, not a fifth-century Briton), so the comedian being in recognisable modern clothes will bridge the gap for us, and for the rest of the clothes the designer can be let loose (within the confines of his or her budget) to create what will convey the fifth century, or certainly ancient times to the audience, while not being so distractingly astounding that people spend time looking at the costumes and trying to work out whether people are dressed richly or poorly, in or out of fashion, instead of listening and responding to what the actors are doing and saying. This is sometimes a difficulty with very elaborate and beautifully designed productions; the eye tends to wander, admiring all the decoration, while the human activity takes second place. After all, as audience, we have only one chance to hear what's said and to notice what the action is. Just like life really!

The vigour of the language will dictate the style of speaking; some of the text reads like pantomime script. For example:

EDWIN: Now, Toclio, what stirring news at Court?

TOCLIO: Oh my Lord, the Court's all filled with rumour, the City with news, and the Country with wonder, and all the bells i'th'Kingdom must proclaim it, we have a new Holy-day a coming.

The dialogue at the opening of the play is in fast one-liners:

CONSTANTIA: I was content to give him wordes for Oathes, he swore so oft he loved me.

DONOBERT: That thou believest him?

CONSTANTIA: He is a man I hope.

DONOBERT: That's in the trial Girl.

CONSTANTIA: However I am a woman, sir.

DONOBERT: The Law's on thy side then, sha't have a Husband and a worthy one: take her, brave Cornwall and make our happiness great as our wishes.

CADOR: Sir, I thank you.

Good economical stuff; gets the plot over briskly. When King Aurelius arrives on the scene, the next speech becomes more decorated, as befits a monarch; but his opening words none-the-less move the action forward, and give information clearly:

AURELIUS: No tiding of our brother yet?

The description of the Hermit's miraculous aid to the British Army, and the subsequent defeat of the Saxons, is couched in rather more dignified, poetic terms than the conversational tone of the first gossipy and family scenes, but the information is still plainly presented for the audience to enjoy the plot. No Shakespearian word-music or images to decorate the thoughts; just robust scene-setting and character introduction.

And suddenly a surprise. The trumpets sound to announce the approach of the Saxon Ambassadors, come to parley peace terms from their British victors. But instead of a gnarled general, a senior politician, a venerable elder or a worthy statesman – a woman, she's the most beautiful, alluring woman ever seen by any of the Britons. The appearance of this dazzling beauty is greeted, not by speeches of poetic appreciation, nor of political oratory, but by old Donobert (the Polonius figure) saying:

> What's here, a woman Orator?

There follows a very comic/dramatic scene in which Aurelius keeps trying to deliver the harsh terms of peace to the representative of his defeated enemy, but finds himself mentioning words like 'love' and being unable to recall what had been decided in the council of war, being tongue-tied by the Saxon princess and her honeyed words and dazzling beauty.

AURELIUS: Fair Damsel, oh my Tongue turns Traitor,
and will betray my heart, sister to our enemy:
's death her beauty mazes me, I cannot speak if I but look on her.

[To DONOBERT] What's that we did conclude?

[DONOBERT starts to speak firmly]

DONOBERT: This Royal Lord...

AURELIUS: Pish, thou canst not utter it: fairs't of creatures, tell the King your Brother that we in Love – ha! and Honor to our country, command his armies to depart our Realm: [He can concentrate no further, begins to woo again] but if you please, fair soul – Lord Donobert, deliver you our pleasure.

But when he does so, in brisk terms, Aurelius rushes to the defence of the princess. The courtiers are appalled. The princess speaks in grossly flattering honeyed words which deceive only somebody under a spell; in this case Aurelius, changed in a matter of thirty lines of dialogue from a strong king into a gibbering romantic fool. Within another page he has proposed marriage to Artesia, the Saxon princess, which throws the court into even greater upheaval. The Hermit arrives to blast the idea of this unholy alliance. But even the strong disapproval and warnings of the Hermit, Saviour of the Britons, cannot move the King from his enchantment with the princess, and the scene ends with a Royal command for Revels to be prepared for the double celebration of the wedding and the new peace treaty. The Courtiers are deeply appalled; the country is about to be allied to its deadliest enemy, and their King is in thrall to a patently evil woman.

Now comes a mirror scene. From one enchanted by lust and beauty, to one enchanted by another kind of devotion.

MODESTIA: I am in love.

HERMIT: In Love, with what?

MODESTIA: With Vertue?

HERMIT: There's no blame in that.

But Modestia's obsession seems to be with the Hermit himself; the kind of evangelical fervour that's almost sexual? The Hermit promises to instruct his new pupil, and the first stirrings indicated of the upheaval of all the family plans arranged in the first scene. The game's afoot! Rowley's Act I ends with plots expounded and order threatened. Meanwhile...

We're removed to a wood. In which two forlorn figures wander. The Clown (alias our comedian) and his extremely pregnant sister, Joan Go-too't. In which we discover that Joan was accosted in this very wood during 'the last great hunting' and as a result of meeting a gentleman – 'He had most rich Attire, a fair Hat and Feather, a gilt Sword, and most excellent hangers.' You'll be happy to know that the 'Hangers' remark is the same as our modern joke. The hangers were part of the accoutrements of the sword belts and buckles. The brother and sister duologue is funny and fast. Bear in mind that the Clown is the leading part in the play. He (and his sister) ramble through all the facets of the various plots and hold the play together. But then, Will Rowley wrote it for himself to play, we assume, and he was the popular comedian the audience would come to see. What your Hollywood moguls call the 'bankable name'. For our modern production this will be the case – the Comedian/Clown will be a well-known comedic name. It will be Roy Hudd, that marvellous comedian in all media; I've worked with him in his great radio shows *Huddlines* and *Huddwinks*, and played Shakespeare with him at the Young Vic and at the National Theatre of Belgium. The play was *Much Ado About Nothing*. I played Beatrice, and he played Dogberry; on television we played in my comedy series *Hold The Front Page*. He's also a great expert and chronicler of the great days of Music Hall and Variety; you'll find his chapter elsewhere in this book, discussing the modern actor's approach to comedy material that was written for an audience centuries ago.

We'll sometimes have to find equivalent or substitute jokes in this play, but not as many as in Shakespeare's Clown's material, which was very often highly topical, slangy, and dependent on puns which no longer mean anything because of different pronunciations of words nowadays. For example; in *The Two Gentlemen of Verona* there's a crosstalk scene which depends for the agility of the argument on the wordplay between 'ship' and 'sheep'. Hard-working actors struggle and wrestle with this to get a laugh. Imagine my interest when in Newfoundland I discovered a clue to the way it originally worked. Newfoundland boasts a way of speaking believed by some to be the closest still existing to the Elizabethan pronunciation of words. Hubert Granter, a very friendly Newfoundlander, was showing me round the town of St John, with its famous harbour. He pointed to the harbour mouth: 'All the big sheeps come in here from all over the world,' he said. So that was how the word was pronounced! And that's why *The Two Gentlemen of Verona* crosstalk had worked originally; not because one person misunderstood the other, but because of the fact that both used the same word with two meanings. But unless the audience knows that as well, the modern actor still has to find a way of making it work for our ears. I seem to remember a routine from an old (1940s?) gramophone record where the problem was the difference between the luggage compartment of a car and an item of footwear; one comic says to the other in exasperation 'When I say boot . . .' 'Yes?' 'I don't mean boot.' 'No?' 'I mean boot!' Old routines are the best.

Mr Granter also illuminated another Shakespeare pun for me. We were driving down a street lined with beautiful old houses, now turned into offices. 'All the liars in town live in this street,' he told me. The liars? 'How do you know that?' I asked. He looked at me as if I was a worm that had crawled out of his hamburger. 'Well, they all have their offices here, the liars, the attorneys, all the legal people.' Ah! Knowing Shakespeare's many references to lawyers, there must have been many an Elizabethan guffaw that passes us by. However, back to the Clown and Joan in the woods where a voice is heard, straining to create romantic poetry dedicated to an unknown beauty. Could this voice belong to Joan's gentleman? Will he be the man they seek – the father of the soon-to-be-born child? The man is revealed to be Prince Uter, the missing brother of King Aurelius (What tidings of our brother? Act I). We can hear distant cries of the search parties looking for Uter. He is clearly in the grip of a romantic vision, his verse is overblown and forlornly lush. It may be that in the production we shall set his love poetry to music. Who can resist lines like these –

PRINCE UTER: You weeping leaves,
    Upon whose tender cheeks doth stand
    A flood of tears at my complaint
    And heard my vows and oaths . . . ?

But no! Joan Go-too't is not the lady of his dreams; he finds her more of a 'Witch! Stallion! Hag!' As the Clown observes: 'I see he will marry her, he speaks so like a husband.' Prince Uter is in process of hitting Joan and her brother to get rid of them and their peculiar accusations, when a courtier we met in Act I appears, attracted by the noise. (This courtier may be an example of economy in our production; two or three characters will have to be melted into one all-purpose courtier.) He in turn is quizzed by the Clown and Joan – is he the father of the child? He, with courtly flattery claims to have seen her pretty face before. This is enough to make her faint. When she recovers, he's gone. So she and her placidly patient brother set off to follow their investigations to Court. Here we'll add a short remark or two about the Comedian's dilemma of finding himself trapped inside this story.

Six days later and the wedding of King Aurelius to Artesia the Saxon princess is in full celebration; we see Ostorius, her brother,

## The Childe hath found his Father

and the formidable figure of Proximus, the Saxon magician. It's in my mind that we'll introduce an example of his magic powers here. We'll have the advice of an illusionist to create some dazzling effects, which I won't discuss here for fear of spoiling the surprise. As the Royals withdraw into an inner room, we hear the Court gossip, and the chorus of disapproval of the royal match; and are introduced to Edol the fiery Earl of Chester, a British military man with a very short fuse. When greeted by all with the friendly 'Welcome to Court, brave Earl,' he replies: 'Do not deceive me by your flatteries; Is not the Saxon here? the League confirm'd? the Marriage ratifi'd? the Court divided with Pagan Infidels? Oh the gods! it is a thought that takes away my sleep and dulls my senses so I scarcely know you: Prepare my horses, Ile away to Chester.'

Later in the play he becomes even terser; during the big battle towards the end of Act IV, he encounters Uter in the full, eloquent flow of a major speech. 'What?' cries Edol, 'Stand you talking? Fight!' He's a very engaging character, Edol, and shares with the other Rowley inventions a kind of comic anarchy mixed with grand dramatic moments. He announces that he will oppose the Saxons till death, and goes to form a Resistance movement with the stirring exit line: 'For in this League, all our whole Kingdom bleeds, which I'd prevent, or perish.'

The wedding feast is subsiding into gloom. The Hermit refuses to drink a health, the atmosphere is tense (and no doubt, drunk!). The Saxon magician called upon to demonstrate his magic powers conjures Achilles and Hector in mortal combat as palpable spirits and apparitions. This effect is ruined by the Hermit stepping between them, and, as he vanquished the Saxon troops with this heavenly fire, he banishes the spirits, who are afeard of him. The Saxon magician is far from pleased, but before the atmosphere deteriorates further, Prince Uter arrives at Court; the lost brother restored, great happiness until – oh no, the beauty to whom Uter made his verses, and pines for, is none other than his brother's new wife! You really can't complain about this plot, can you? And before many more moments have passed, a gift is secretly brought to Uter from Artesia, who, although newly married, is already making an assignation with her husband's brother. Why? The Act ends on the cliffhanger of Uter's predicament:

UTER: Vices are vertues, if so thought and seen,
    And trees with foulest roots branch soonest green.

And that's the end of Rowley's Act II; our Act I, since I plan to present the play in three acts for our audience; that is to stay, Rowley's Acts I and II become our Act I, his Act III is our Act II, and his Acts IV and V become our Act III. Two intervals.

**Act II**

Rowley's Act III begins with a scene between Clown and Sister, still on the trail, hunting for the Father of the Childe. By the way, there's a line in Shakespeare's *Winter's Tale*, where the Old Shepherd, discovering a baby abandoned in a remote place, asks 'A boy or a child, I wonder?' I've known actors wrestle with that line; then in Devon one time I heard someone in our village ask the same question of a proud new uncle celebrating in a pub. Child means girl in that context; but in Rowley's title Childe is a generic term for unborn baby. Meanwhile, back in Act III . . .

It's in my mind to start with the Comedian escaping momentarily from the fifth century, and telling the audience of his off-stage encounters with Saxons and their ways. Bob Stewart has written a very good song entitled 'What do the Saxons do?' This is very much a singalong song in the pantomime tradition.

The song ends in a sudden black-out and return to the fifth century. An image is seen of Joan Go-too't asleep on a hill. A cloaked figure with feathered hat on head approaches through the mist. Joan awakes, cries out with pleasure, she embraces the cloaked figure to sweet music playing. 'My sweet friend!' she says. Black-out. Lights up to reveal her in the arms of the Clown, who is shaking her awake. They arrive at Court, and meet many of the people we already know, and another courtier, Sir Nicodemus Nothing (I imagine this name is pronounced 'No-thing' as in 'Much Ado about . . .'). The Clown questions everybody closely, suspecting every feather-hatted man he meets, desperate to find the father and get on with his own life. He's now lost patience. In the scene with Nicodemus there's a 'conning' sequence about money that's in our pantomime tradition of city slicker v country bumpkin. Left with no money, no hope of finding the father, and a violent storm brewing, the Clown is going to abandon Joan, but is stopped (by Merlin's influence?): 'I think I am bewitch with thee, I cannot finde in my heart to forsake her.' The storm threatens. 'Thunder. Enter the Devil in man's habit, richly attired, his feet and his head horrid.' [Horrid (archaic or poetic) shaggy, bristling, rough; (colloquial) repellent, detestable.]

Joan hails her sweet friend. At last, she's found him! But he's invisible to the Clown, although he can hear the Devil's voice. Joan runs off, following the Devil, followed by the Clown, who thinks she's run mad.

## The Childe hath found his Father

The next scenes concern the further adventures of Modestia, now set upon a life of piety; reneging on her marriage promise to Edwin, and disrupting her sister's wedding procession, and persuading Constantia to join her in a religious life: the outraged bridegroom calls on the Bishop to insist that the wedding go ahead. The Bishop: 'Her self gives barr, my Lord, to your desires, and our performance; 'tis against the Law and Orders of the Church to force a Marriage.'

A very nasty family row breaks out, and the dispute rages off into the distance. Now the upset of Nature continues with thunder and lightning and the Devil erupting onto the scene, with powerful incantations, bringing forth the Fates, and Lucina, Queen of Night, who (in our production) sings the incantations of the merits and gifts to be showered on the newly being born child, giving him his name 'Merlin' and since he was born in the forest (where Joan had followed the Devil after the last scene in which we saw her) the Fates have named him Merlin Silvester.

The Fates weave their cords of life in the traditional colours of black, red and white (Bob Stewart can explain that), the magical effects reach the zenith of their power and impressiveness; the Devil vanishes amid thunder. Here's the Clown: 'Well, I wonder how my poor sister does, after all this thundering . . .' And here, at last, is the eponymous hero of the play: Merlin arrives, reading a book. He looks 'like an artichoke' and sports a very full head of golden red hair and a beard, and is extremely tall for his age (five minutes). Joan is thrilled with her son, but wonders why he fixes his eyes so deeply on the book. Merlin's first words: 'To sound the depth of Arts, of Learning, Wisdom, Knowledge'. There. He's done that. Now to meet his family. And to introduce his uncle to his father ('He keeps a Hot-house 'ith' Low Countries'), and there's a general happy family atmosphere, with the Clown blissfully unaware that his new unofficial brother-in-law is the Devil; although a suspicion creeps into his mind after the Devil's vision of the future and his abrupt disappearance . . . 'though he hide his horns with his hat and feather, I spi'd his cloven hoof for all his cunning.' Merlin and his family set off for the doomed castle of Vortigern, King 'of the Welch Britons', there to begin the first of the great adventures.

Others are heading towards Vortigern's castle. Ostorious the Saxon king sends his magician Proximus to propose an alliance between the Saxons (now supposed friends-by-marriage of the Britons) and Vortigern; a treachery foreseen by the Devil. There's also a plot to kill Aurelius and his brother, and that's been planned by Artesia. The first move in her plot is to seduce Prince Uter, who struggles against her sweet talk, and resists all her seduction. But Artesia screams for help, cries Rape, and on cue the Saxon faction arrive, 'to rescue the Queen'. The Britons arrive to defend their king's brother, refusing to believe a word the Saxons say. A family row on the scale of a small war breaks out. Words like 'pernicious rat!' and 'low-bred despicable creeper, insulting Toad' are exchanged. But the Saxons win, with Aurelius the British king still in thrall to his enchanting wife. 'Since Brittain fails', he tells his loyal, bewildered courtiers, 'we'll trust to forrain [i.e. Saxon] friends, and guard our person from your traitorous ends.'

The Act ends with all the various strands of the plot converging towards one place: 'To Wales!'

## ACT III

Rowley's Act IV. I plan to begin the Act with a vision of the doomed castle of Vortigern seen collapsing in flames with the prophecy spoken:

> King Vortigern's castle can never stand
> Till the foundation's laid with mortar
> Temper'd with the fatal blood of such a childe
> Whose father was no mortal.

There's only one person who fits that job description. Merlin in danger! But here he is, untroubled, with his assistant spirit. (In our production it'll have to be a puppet operated by the actor playing Merlin; in Rowley's time it would have been, like the other 'sprites' in the play, a child actor. Child actors cost a great deal in modern productions; they very often have to be double cast, they have to have a chaperone, and sometimes a tutor, so that they can continue their schooling during rehearsal.) Merlin and his glove-puppet spirit are engaged in picking the Clown's pocket. With the help of the illusionist, we can have a very funny sequence here; interrupted by two gentlemen, sent by Vortigern to search for the 'fiend begotten child'. The Clown's instinct is to protect his nephew, but Merlin is confident: 'Uncle, your perswasion must not prevail with me, I know mine enemies better than you do.'

Now the play begins a new phase, all action, magic, adventure, prophecy; and starts its fast-paced climb to the climax, with Merlin taking over as the main power-house of the playing. This is an interesting feature of the many-faceted play – the main character doesn't appear until Act III of Rowley's play, and brings a whole new energy to the latter part of the entertainment, like fresh troops arriving at a battle. This is the section of the play where the Director, the Designer, the Lighting Designer, the Composer, and the Illusionist have to pool their resources and ideas, because the technical demands are many and complex (examples: aerial battle of red and white dragons; comet with seven points of light).

Another byway – the comet so carefully described in the play – 'this fiery exaltation shoots his frightful horrors on th'amazed world, see in the beam that 'bout his flaming ring, a Dragon's head appears, from out whose mouth two flaming slakes of fire, stretch East and West . . .' was mentioned recently (1 October 1988) in the *Daily Telegraph*. In the 'Space' section of that paper is quoted the following description: 'The fire of righteous vengeance, kindled by the sins of the past, blazed from sea to sea and burned up the whole surface of the island.' This attributed to Gildas, British historian of the Dark Ages, describing the fifth century. And the article accompanying the quotation told of Dr Victor Clube an Oxford physicist, who identifies the 'blazing star' as being the Comet Encke, which he believes to have last sent devastating particles to Earth as late as 1908, in Siberia. A block of ice, about forty yards wide and weighing some thirty thousand tons, being a detached fragment from Comet Encke, caused an explosion equivalent to a nuclear bomb of between ten and twenty megatons. Two thousand five hundred square miles of forest were flattened, wrote Adrian Berry in his article about Encke and Dr Clube's theory that the comet is far from harmless even now; and along with some ten thousand million other comets in space, could be a threat to our planet. That's all we need.

An astonishing comet was a prominent feature of the sixteenth-century play *The Revenger's Tragedy*, which I saw at Theatr Clwyd this year, again a Toby Robertson production, again splendid. I was particularly impressed with the design of the production, and found it had been created by someone I had worked with over twenty years ago. Alan Barrett had been Costume Designer for the film *Far from the Madding Crowd*, in which I played a small part. At the time of writing this chapter Alan and I are engaged in preliminary thinking and scribbling and discussing ideas, visions and practical suggestions for *The Birth of Merlin*; Bob Stewart and I have discussed and planned the musical structure of the production, and the three of us have met together to confer and continue the preparation of the production.

Soon casting decisions will have to be made; financial limits set; lighting and technical plans prepared; and of course, the all-important decision: will the production go ahead? By the time the play reaches the point of being seen by the audience in the theatre, the work of nearly one hundred people will be involved. A big undertaking; and if you feel I've harped on the financial theme too much, I'm afraid that's what the facts of theatre life have always been – even for Messrs Shakespeare and Rowley.

But away with mundane things – what's happening to Merlin? Our hero conquers Proximus the Saxon magician with a fatal prophecy. The stage instruction for the death of Proximus is nearly as good as the famous *'Exit pursued by a bear'* in *the Winter's Tale*. In our play 'a stone falls and kills Proximus', who dies laughing. The Clown is immediately worried – 'Cousin Merlin, there's no more of this stone fruit ready to fall, is there? I pray you, give your Uncle a little fair warning.' Battle is joined between Edol with the supporters of Prince Uter, and Vortigern's forces; urged on by Edol, with Uter advising counsel. But warlike emotions prevail and a fierce battle is fought, with Edol in full cry; a final confrontation between Uter and Vortigern interrupted by the fiery Edol who takes upon himself the despatch of Vortigern, driving him into the castle. The blazing comet appears. Who can interpret this heavenly portent?

Now Merlin takes over the action, with prophecy immediate (the death by poison of Aurelius at the hands of Artesia and the Saxons) and the future rulers of Brittain. He rescues his mother from the hated clutches of the Devil and his minions, and imprisons the Devil within a rock; he promises his mother a monument for all time: 'I will erect a Monument upon the verdant Plains of Salisbury, no King shall have so high a sepulchre, with pendulous stones that I will hang by art, where neither lime nor mortar shall be us'd, a dark Enigma to the memory, for none shall have the power to number them, a place that I will hollow for your rest, Where no night-hag shall walk, nor Ware-wolf tread, Where Merlin's mother shall be sepulcher'd.' He silences the Clown by striking him dumb, in the style of *The Magic Flute* and many other legends. But Will Rowley wouldn't stay silent for long. The Clown's 'hum hum hum' is as eloquent as his usual conversation, and just as disrupting.

The wicked princess comes to a satisfyingly bad end – 'she shall be buried circled in a wall' – and goes to her doom unrepentant and defiant: 'Thy brother's poisoned but I wanted more!' Prince Uter (now named Pendragon) comes to maturity, and sees Merlin's vision of the future line of kings. The play ends in a patriotic tableau of great splendour. The one unresolved plot is that of the two bridegrooms jilted at the altar by their brides having been seduced by the life religious. Remember them? Rowley shoves a short scene into the action as the penultimate moment of the play. It may be that he's quite right, but I feel that the little 'pay-off' scene would fit better

*The Childe hath found his Father*

as a swift epilogue, leaving the big patriotic build-up to progress unhindered. So that's what we'll try. With a return to the Comedian and his bewilderment – still locked in time into the middle of the joke he was telling at the start of the evening. Had he seen the things he thought he'd seen? What had happened to him? He was standing here when these people . . . and here they are again. Donobert, Gloster, Cador and Edwin, in conversation, crossing the stage, resolving the last strand of plot: 'Let my old arms embrace, and call you Sons; for by the Honor of my father's House, I'le part my estate most equally betwixt you,' says Donobert. 'Sir, y'are most noble!' the two young men reply. And from the pleased expressions we glean that they are now young millionaires, as they all disappear.

The Comedian wants to follow them. Behind that curtain is the whirling space in which all the strange adventures happen. He instructs the curtain to be raised so that he can show us what he means. But what is revealed is – I won't spoil the effect, you'll just have to see the production!

We've left the text for you to read in as close a form as possible to the original – you'll see from the facsimile on page 64 how densely printed the original is; and how trying for our ignorant eyes with the 's' seemingly printed as 'f'. All we've done is to have the text printed clearly, but not arranged it into an edited version, so that you can have the pleasure of reading the seventeenth-century dialogue, and find the verse emerging from the prose. The language isn't too obscure – words like 'Jug' (the nickname for Joan, used by the Clown) can be found in the *Dictionary of Archaic Phrase*. Apparently Jug was the usual familiar form of Joan, like Tel for Terry and Del for Derek nowadays. The word also means 'a pasture used by all'. No comment.

There was just one word, 'diggon', which I couldn't find in any list, but the meaning is clear within the Clown's speech; I wonder if that word found its way to the Americas to become 'doggone'? It seems to be a phrase meaning to cancel out, as used in the Clown's text. See what you think. I hope you enjoy reading the text as a new play; mostly we come to old texts that have already been edited, commented on, and rearranged by academics for many centuries and with many conflicting theories. As you'll have gathered from this chapter, I'm no academic, and this summary of the play is simply my personal reaction as a working director preparing a production. My duty is to reveal the play for a twentieth-century audience, as entertainingly and as clearly as I can; giving the actors the greatest opportunity to shine and show their talent to the very height of their powers; and to be responsible to the management for the overall spending of their money. The director isn't a dictator, simply the person who constantly keeps the whole production in mind, who arranges the work of the many people who create the play for the audience to the best advantage of all concerned.

In conclusion I can only quote the original frontispiece of 1662: 'Placere cupio' . . . and hope that before long Merlin will be reborn and 'acted with great applause'.

# HE MAY HAVE BEEN SHORT, BUT . . .
## Roy Hudd
### (with interruptions by *Bob Stewart*)

*Prologue* Once upon a time a comedian/actor and an author/composer sat down together to talk about a play. The author was a very serious type, who was certain that the play was all about Celtic mythology, mysticism, and similar obscure subjects. The comedian soon put him right.

**Roy** *The Birth of Merlin* is full of gags – it's written by an experienced working comic or clown, Will Rowley. Lots of the gags are still used regularly today, even if the exact details vary or are a little modernised, and I'll bet that they were used in Roman times, too. Shakespeare himself used lots of what were, already in his time, old gags. But people in show business always say 'why use that old gag?'. Well, I use them because they're good gags. Like good wine, they mature with age, and as long as they still get big laughs, why not. Anyway, if it was good enough for Shakespeare, it ought to be good enough for anyone. I'm sure Rowley thought that way too, though he drew his gags from far and wide just like any good comedian today does. Because we find a gag or a sketch in Will Shakespeare, then later in Will Rowley, and the same gag later again by the great Dan Leno and many others, most definitely does *not* mean that they are all copies of Shakespeare. The humour, the situations, the gags themselves, are very often traditional, and go back a long way before any first known version. It's the individual skill at working them into a play or a show, of course, that is the hallmark of greatness. And nobody can beat Shakespeare at that.

But Will Rowley did a pretty good job himself; take the first scene of *The Birth of Merlin*, built around the situation of Joan's pregnancy, and a typical old gag, the business with the *hangers*. There are dozens of jokes that substitute objects, maps, plants, puns and the like for parts of the human body. Its the substitution that's funny, not the parts themselves, though Joan of course misses the point altogether and is very straight while the Clown plays the gag for everything it's worth.

**Bob** That hangers joke is found in another form in *Hamlet*, (Act 5, Scene 2), when Hamlet mocks the over-serious Osric.

**Roy** Hangers? It's like Trossachs isn't it?

**Bob** Pardon?

**Roy** He ran away to Scotland but was caught by the Trossachs! Or if that's too geographic, then you could say he was trapped by the constables!

There was a popular variety comedian just after the war, called Leon Cortez, who used to specialise in potted Shakespeare. 'There was this geezer, see, and he was a snotty so and so, nothing made him happy, but he did enjoy a feel yah see. No, no, no, *Ophelia* see, that was the name of his bit of crumpet . . .' Now Leon Cortez used to get the whole plot of *Hamlet* across in about three minutes, so once again it's not only the content, but the way it's put together that counts.

But the real point about *The Birth of Merlin* is that it has all the elements of a pantomime. There are really black hearted villains, wizards, shining white heroes, and of course it has four great comic spots. That's very significant. That's what you, or at least *I* would do when I put a panto together. I go in and say, I do the opening, the kitchen scene, the automation scene, which can be a four or five handed sketch, and I do one with the kids at the end. I do the 'not 'ere' gag, and the Tree of Truth gag . . .

**Bob** The knot ear gag?

**Roy** Well, you've almost got it, it's a comic and straight man sketch. It goes like this:

S M: Ah, there are you Jack!

C: I'm here

S M: And so am I

C: Oh no you're not

S M: I most certainly am!

C: You're not, you know.

S M: What are you talking about?

C: I say you're not 'ere.

S M: Well of course I am. Aren't I boys and girls?
  (Audience) Yes!

C: Oh no he's not!

And Oh yes he is (etcetera).

C: Right, I'll prove to you that you're not 'ere. In fact I bet you a pound that I can!

S M: You're on . . . here's my pound,

C: Right, now, you're not in Edinburgh, are you?

S M: No, I'm not in Edinburgh.

C: Good, and you're not in Cardiff, are you?

S M: No, I'm not in Cardiff.

C: Well if you're not in Edinburgh and you're not in Cardiff, you must be somewhere else!

S M: Correct!

C: Well, if you're somewhere else . . . you're not 'ere! (Takes the money and runs.)

That's a Joe Grimaldi gag, like the Tree of Truth. Grimaldi was the great clown of the nineteenth century. There's something similar to the Tree of Truth in our play, you know the idea, if you tell a lie an apple will fall on your head. Only for Proximus it's a dirty great stone and it kills him!

**Bob** Do you think the play really works for a modern audience?

**Roy** Of course it does, providing you don't mess around with it. You can't 'improve' on classic comedy. You don't muck around with stuff like that, and that's its strength, that's why it survives through the centuries.

**Bob** Interesting . . . that's what I always say about the old Merlin legends, you can't improve upon or interfere with a tradition. They're woven together with the classic comedy in the play.

**Roy** But if someone did try to improve on these legends, they'd ruin them, wouldn't they? That's what we always say to young performers in pantomime when we rehearse the gags. It's the simplicity that counts, never try to improve on the simple old form, always stick to it. The old gags have their own rhythms, and if you change them to be clever you weaken them. The gags in *The Birth of Merlin* have those same recognisable rhythms. You can tell that a comic or clown, or whatever he would have been called in the seventeenth century when it was performed, put the play together; classic gags, classic rhythms, and four great solo spots between the spectacular action.

Those four spots are in the right places; just when you think things are getting heavy and complicated, on come the double act, Clown and Joan, just like George Burns and Gracie Allen. In fact the double act in the play is very similar, where she is the daft one.

**Bob** So how far apart is Rowley's Clown, or his double act with Joan, from a modern act?

**Roy** I think that they're pretty close – though the play is much stronger in its content because she's pregnant . . . so a lot of the action is stronger than in a family show or modern pantomime, for example. A lot of the humour is that kind of bawdy suggestive stuff that carried right through Variety and the Music Halls: 'Believe me brother,' says Joan innocently, or perhaps stupidly, 'he was a gentleman!' And there she is, with her big belly: and Will Rowley was fat too, because he described himself and her as two Great Britons.

So in that sense it's cruder than the modern panto, more earthy, and modern panto is for families so you expect it to be less strong in its humour. But the basic format is till the same as a pantomime, despite the strength of the gags or situations.

**Bob** One thought that occurred to me as I worked on the play was who might have played Joan, Merlin's mum. I mean, we don't know for sure if Joan Go-too't was a man or a woman. Rowley's time was a time of transition in performing.

**Roy** That's right. We know that boys played the female roles in the earlier plays such as Shakespeare. But I think that Joan behaves a lot like a Dame in pantomime, which means that she was a man in drag. She's similar to Jack's mother in *Jack and the Beanstalk*, and even more like *Mother Goose* who starts of as a silly old cow and then becomes beautiful.

**Bob** Which is exactly what happens to Joan!

**Roy** Ah but when Mother Goose becomes beautiful she becomes horrid and pretentious; Joan becomes beautiful and stays that way. *Mother Goose* was supposed to have been written for Dan Leno the great Victorian pantomime comic, between 1880 and 1890. But I wouldn't be at all surprised if it tapped in to an older tradition, such as we find with Joan Go-too't. If you think about it, it's too broad to have a boy playing Joan, like those who played the female roles in Shakespeare. In Rowley's time I guess that Joan would have been a big strapping man with false boobs and belly.

Today of course, we have a different situation. You still have the pantomime Dame, who is a man, and the principal boy, who is a girl. But we also have some great comediennes, such as Anna Karen who'll be Joan to my Clown.

**Bob** Might not Will Rowley have had a lady to work with?

**Roy** I think it would have been too strong in those days. Even today there are things that a Dame can do in pantomime because she's a man. They wouldn't work with a lady Dame, they'd just be offensive. But for our play, a strong woman will be perfect for Joan. After all, this is almost the twenty-first century!

**Bob** This play is clearly one where a star, well known to his audience, wraps the action round himself, as you said. Is this a well established working situation in comedy, in pantomime, in other dramas? Who else comes to mind, apart from Dan Leno who you mentioned earlier?

**Roy** Well, we still work that way today, it hasn't changed too much. Norman Wisdom plays pantomimes with four big feature spots, and you just wrap the rest of the show around him. Recently Russ Abbott was in panto, in *Jack and the Beanstalk*, and had to do his popular characters who we've all seen on television. That's his act. And I think that Rowley did a lot of business, a lot of visual things that were part of his act, and not necessarily noted in the script.

When I played Andrew Aguecheek in *Twelfth Night* there was an indication in the text, something like 'comedy swordfight here!' Well that by itself doesn't help much, but Shakespeare gave the comics a lot to work on. In *Twelfth Night*, before we come to the note about the swordfight, he has established that the two protagonists area cowardly simpleton, Aguecheek, and a girl in drag, who has never held a sword let alone fought a duel . . . what scope for comedy business that gives you!

But Rowley must have done a lot of visual things, perhaps gags that were popular with the London audience already, which he had made famous. Take the bit where he is struck dumb by Merlin. It's not much in the script, but it must have been a special act, perhaps he was a good mime and the crowd expected this feature spot from him.

**Bob** So what other clown springs to mind in this context?

**Roy** Well, Joe Grimaldi was one of the greatest. He had established routines, the pantomime of his days was actually advertised as 'Jack and the Beanstalk – in which Mr Grimaldi will sing his famous song *Hot Codlins*'. Perhaps a playbill of *The Birth of Merlin* would have read 'In which Mr Rowley will do his famous dumb show.' After all, he's only struck dumb for a brief moment in the script, it reads like nothing at all. But it has to be a special feature in performance, a great solo for the Clown.

**Bob** But there's also a team; he has people with him, which suggests that he had a regular team.

**Roy** Just like the Crazy Gang or the Marx Brothers, or even Hilda Baker and her daughter Cynthia, who was a big tall dopey man in drag. But Rowley's team would have been fairly small, just himself

## The Birth of Merlin

as Clown, Joan and then Merlin. The rest of the company would have been working actors. We still do this today, where the comics bounce off the serious actors and make a mockery of them. Sometimes this becomes a feature in its own right; that's why famous serious actors appear as guests in comedy shows. I can see this happening quite successfully in the original performances of *The Birth of Merlin*.

**Bob** How much would the rest of the company have ad-libbed; the original play is in blank verse, very tightly written and well organised. I'm thinking now of the famous speech, again in *Hamlet* where improvising is seriously criticised. Obviously Shakespeare had suffered at the hands of a clown who ran off with certain scenes . . .

**Roy** Yes, well that was probably Will Kemp, the famous clown who worked with Shakespeare. He originated the phrase 'A Nine Days Wonder', which he used to advertise his Morris Dance from London to Norwich. In *The Birth of Merlin* I don't think that the company would have improvised, and I don't think that all three of Rowley's own team would have ad-libbed either.

The freedom would have been mainly given to the clown, the star. Think of Will Hay playing headmaster, where he could improvise freely but his team had a very strict script to work to. This is one of the most tried and proven methods of successful comedy, and it happens repeatedly in our play. Like Jimmy James, who also ad-libbed freely while his team stayed on script. Another example was Arthur Haines, where the improvising seemed, deceptively to get out of hand, but his straight man, Nicholas Parsons, always brought things back into line.

Now that's exactly what Joan does, believe it or not, she brings it all back into line and on to the next sequence every time. She always comes in with the next feed line: 'believe me brother he was a gentleman', setting us up ready for the Clown's gag.

**Bob** The dumb scene that you mentioned earlier is found in other sources too: *The Magic Flute*, and I'm thinking particularly of the Welsh legend of Taliesin, where a young poet or magical child, similar in many ways to the youthful Merlin, goes to the king's court. He strikes all the bards dumb with his power, and all that they can say is 'Blrwm, blrwm, blrwm', like the Clown's 'Hum, hum, hum' in *The Birth of Merlin*. Perhaps it is an ancient motif?

**Roy** I expect you could have found it in the theatres of Greece or Rome. Some of the gags in Shakespeare's *Comedy of Errors* go right back to the Roman playwright Plautus. He was a great inventor of comedies . . . the popular musical *A Funny Thing Happened On The Way To The Forum* was based upon several of his plots. In fact, Shakespeare nicked the plot of a Plautus play, *The Menechmi* for

*Comedy of Errors*; the original Roman play had only one set of twins, but he added a second set and in one stroke created four double acts instead of two, and built up the wife and her sister Luciana into yet a fifth two hander. Once again, it's the way you handle the traditional material that counts, not looking for any specific source.

There's another old gag that is similar to the dumb show, one which I do every year in pantomime: its called The Magic Hat Routine. When the hat is on someone's head they can't hear a thing. Of course really the comic's miming and then when he lifts the hat he comes in out loud with something outrageous or ridiculous as if the straight man has suddenly got his hearing back. All of these miming comedy routines go back to ancient times, I'm sure.

The other important feature of *The Birth of Merlin* is the knock-about stuff, which was, incidentally, quite violent in Shakespeare, or Rowley's day. The word 'slapstick' is used for almost any kind of physical comedy nowadays, but originally it was a special 'slap-stick', which doesn't hurt much, but makes a terrific sound, and that's what sets the audience laughing. Most of the clowns in the sixteenth and seventeenth centuries were jugglers and tumblers, so some real acrobatics and pratt falls would have been meat and drink to them. Own up, you never hear an audience laugh as loudly at words as they do at Laurel and Hardy, Buster Keaton, and, of course, Charlie Chaplin.

**Bob** You've reminded me of something that Professor Brooks mentioned: Merlin's Rod, found in Malory's *Morte D'Arthur* and also in connection with Prospero in *The Tempest*. I wonder if a slap-stick was used by Merlin when he fought with Proximus that wicked Saxon necromancer?

There's another device that interests me, also mentioned by Professor Brooks, and again found in *Hamlet*. The Devil can be seen by Joan, but not by the Clown.

**Roy** Aha! That is total traditional pantomime: the Harlequin. The audience knew all about this, it was an accepted device, when the Harlequin pointed to one of the diamonds on his costume, and it depended upon the colour indicated, he was always invisible to the other actors. So the audience could see him, but nobody on stage so he could make his mischief unseen. But when he pointed to a different colour on his costume, everyone could see him!

**Bob** And of course the ghost in *Hamlet* does something very similar, appearing only to his son, invisible to everyone else. But that's not at all humorous.

**Roy** But we also have the host gag in pantomime, don't we: 'You will tell me when you see him, boys and girls, won't you?' The same device, different emphasis.

**Bob** What about the scene with Nicodemus Nothing, who tricks the Clown out of money for false legal advice. This is the scenario of the Country Bumpkin and the City Slicker, isn't it?

**Roy** A well-known turn. The Village Idiot who actually scores . . . it's run through every part of theatrical history. Sometimes the humour works when he doesn't score, of course: there's a Comic and Villain gag that we use in pantomime:

*Comic*: Oi! You owe me five pounds!

*Villain*: I'll give you an I.O.U. (gets out piece of paper) Have you got a pencil?

*Comic*: Certainly (gives Villain pencil)

*Villain*: (writing) There – I.O.U. five pounds. Just sign here, will you?

*Comic*: Of course. (signs. Villain takes paper)

*Villain*: Thank you. (goes to exit)

*Comic*: Oi, just a minute! You must think I'm simple. Give us back me pencil!

In *The Birth of Merlin* the Clown gets his legal advice, which is nothing more nor less than whoever the baby calls daddy, challenge him to marry Joan. But this is turned against Nicodemus Nothing, (notice the implication, Nicodemus No-Thing) and he is challenged to marry her. It has the feeling of a well established routine, though I think that the script, again, does not tell us everything that went on.

**Bob** Like the pocket-picking scene, with the little Antic Spirit?

**Roy** Yes indeed. That must have been a special routine. I can see a conjuror coming into play the antic spirit, a professional pocket picker and trickster, who does the tricks that stage magicians still do today. You know, they call up a member of the audience, and steal his watch, his tie, even his braces. That's another feature spot, a threesome playing Find the Lady with the Clown's pockets. You can bet that all sorts of things were done in that scene, and that all kinds of objects came out of his pockets sometimes, too. Exactly the same sort of show might have been done outside the theatre in the London Street by buskers, though criminal pick-pocketing was heavily punished at that time.

**Bob** And then there's the joke about Merlin being small, a little hairy artichoke. There's a lot of implied humour there, and we are set up for it right at the beginning in Scene 1 with all the business about 'short things' and 'hangers'.

**Roy** You're beginning to get the idea now. There was a famous Max Miller gag about the man of five foot one who married a girl of six foot because she got pregnant. How did that happen? Well somebody must have put him up to it! That very gag is found in *The Birth of Merlin*. And what about the place-name puns, where the Clown says that the Go too' its come from *Hockley in the Hole* and *Layton Buzzard*. We still use those puns today, like the conversation on a crowded Tube train: 'Is this Cockfosters?' 'No madam, it's mine!' Or 'Are you going to Clapham?' 'Only if they're very good!'

So the frocks change, but the gags endure. So do the comic characters from Plautus, the medieval Mystery plays, Mummers' Plays, Will Shakespeare, to Will Rowley, of course. Then on to the Music Halls, Variety, and modern pantomime, most of all, pantomime. That's the real key to this play, it's a great roaring pantomime.

By the way, how tall are you?

**Bob**, Blrwm, blrwm, blrwm.

# The BIRTH of MERLIN:
## OR,
## *The Childe hath found his Father.*

### ACTUS. I.

*Enter Donobert, Gloster, Cador, Edwin, Constantia, and Modestia.*

*Cador.* You teach me language, sir, as one that knows the Debt of Love I owe unto their Vertues, wherein like a true Courtier I have fed my self with hope of fair Success, and now attend your wisht consent to my long Suit.

*Dono.* Believe me, youthful Lord, time could not give an opportunity more fitting your desires, always provided my Daughters love be suited with my Grant. *Cador.* 'Tis the condition sir, her Promise seal'd. *Dono.* Ist so, *Constantia?*

*Constan.* I was content to give him words for oathes, he swore so oft he lov'd me. *Dono.* That thou believest him?

*Const.* He is a man I hope. *Dono.* That's in the trial Girl.

*Const.* However I am a woman, sir. *Dono.* The Law's on thy side then, sha't have a Husband, I, and a worthy one: Take her brave *Cornwal*, and make our happiness great as our wishes.

*Cador.* Sir, I thank you. *Glost.* Double the fortunes of the day, my Lord, and crown my wishes too: I have a son here, who in my absence would protest no less unto your other Daughter. *Dono.* Ha *Gloster*, is it so? what says Lord *Edwin?* will she protest as much to thee?

*Edwin.* Else must she want some of her Sisters faith, Sir.

*Modesta.* Of her credulity much rather, Sir: My Lord, you are a Soldier, and methinks the height of that Profession should diminish all heat of Loves desires, being so late employ'd in blood and ruine. *Edwin.* The more my Conscience tyes me to repair

The opening page of the 1662 edition

# The Birth of Merlin

OR

## The Childe hath found his Father

as it has been several times acted
with great applause . . .

Written by William Shakespeare
and William Rowley

*Placere cupio*

---

LONDON Printed by Tho. Johnson for Francis Kirkman,
and Henry March, and are to be sold at the Princes Arms in
Chancery-Lane. 1662

---

*Date of writing uncertain probably c 1620*
*Date of this the earliest and only known edition 1662 (BM C34 17)*
*Reproduced in facsimile 1910.*

# Editorial Note

The text which follows is based upon the 1662 Kirkman and Marsh publication of *The Birth of Merlin*, with a number of amendments as suggested by Professor C. F. Tucker Brooke in his *Shakespeare Apocrypha* (Clarendon Press, 1908). The original play was written entirely in blank verse with occasional rhyming couplets, but the 1662 edition compressed most of the text into blocks of prose, often in a careless manner. This 1989 edition has, therefore, adjusted the typesetting of the play in many places where the 1662 edition has clearly damaged the work of the playwright, but has not attempted a detailed academic reconstruction of the original verses. This edition is intended for modern reading and performance; when the play is read aloud (in any variant or edition) the natural rhythmns and structures of the playwright come alive, and I have felt it sufficient to adjust the text only where such life has been stifled by the 1662 setting.

*R. J. Stewart*

# DRAMMATIS PERSONAE

*The Scene  Brittain*

| | |
|---|---|
| AURELIUS | King of Brittain |
| VORTIGER | King of Brittain |
| UTER PENDRAGON | The Prince, brother to Aurelius |
| DONOBERT | A Nobleman, and father to Constantia and Modestia |
| EARL OF GLOSTER | and Father to Edwyn |
| EDOLL | Earl of Chester and General to King Aurelius |
| CADOR | Earl of Cornwall and Suitor to Constantia |
| EDWIN | Son to the Earl of Gloster and Suitor to Modestia |
| TOCLIO & OSWALD | Two Noblemen |
| MERLIN | The Prophet |
| ANSELME | The Hermit, after Bishop of Winchester |
| CLOWN | Brother to Joan, mother of Merlin |
| SIR NICHODEMUS NOTHING | A Courtier |
| THE DEVIL | Father of Merlin |
| OSTORIUS | The Saxon General |
| OCTA | A Saxon Nobleman |
| PROXIMUS | A Saxon Magician |
| Two Bishops | |
| Two Saxon Lords | |
| Two of Edol's Captains | |
| Two Gentlemen | |
| A little Antick Spirit | |
| ARTESIA | Sister to Ostorius the Saxon General |
| CONSTANTIA & MODESTIA | Daughters to Donobert |
| JOAN GO–TOO'T | Mother of Merlin |
| A WAITING WOMAN | to Artesia |
| LUCINA | Queen of the Shades |

# THE BIRTH OF MERLIN
## Or
## The Childe Hath Found His Father

## ACT I

*Scene 1:* (Enter DONOBERT, GLOSTER, CADOR, EDWIN, CONSTANTIA and MODESTIA)

CADOR: You teach me language, sir, as one that knows the Debt of Love I owe unto their Vertues, wherein like a true Courtier I have fed my self with hope of fair Success, and now attend your wisht consent to my long Suit.

DONOBERT: Believe me, youthful Lord, time could not give an opportunity more fitting your desires, always provided my Daughters love be suited with my Grant.

CADOR: 'Tis the condition sir, her Promise seal'd.

DONOBERT: Ist so, Constantia?

CONSTANTIA: I was content to give him words for oathes, he swore so oft he love'd me.

DONOBERT: That thou believest him?

CONSTANTIA: He is a man I hope.

DONOBERT: That's in the trial Girl.

CONSTANTIA: However I am a woman, sir.

DONOBERT: The Law's on thy side then, sha't have a Husband and a worthy one: Take her brave Cornwal, and make our happiness great as our wishes.

CADOR: Sir, I thank you.

GLOSTER: Double the fortunes of the day, my Lord, and crown my wishes too: I have a son here, who in my absence would protest no less unto your other Daughter.

DONOBERT: Ha Gloster, is it so? what says Lord Edwin? will she protest as much to thee?

EDWIN: Else must she want some of her Sisters faith, Sir.

MODESTIA: Of her credulity much rather, Sir: My Lord, you are a Soldier, and methinks the height of that Profession should diminish all heat of Loves desires, being so late employ'd in blood and ruine.

EDWIN: The more my Conscience tyes me to repair the worlds losses in a new succession.

MODESTIA: Necessity it seems ties your affections then, and at that rate I would unwillingly be thrust upon you, a wife is a dish soon cloys, sir.

EDWIN: Weak and diseased appetites it may.

MODESTIA: Most of your making have dull stomacks sir.

DONOBERT: If that be all Girl, thou shalt quicken him, be kind to him.

MODESTIA: Noble Edwin, let it suffice what's mine in her, speaks yours; For her consent, let your fair suit go on, She is a woman sir, and will be won.

(Enter TOCLIO)

EDWIN: You give me comfort sir.

DONOBERT: Now Toclio.

TOCLIO: The King, my honor'd Lords, requires your presence, and calls a Councel for return of answer unto the parling enemy, whose Embassadors are on the way to Court.

DONOBERT: So suddenly, Chester it seems has ply'd them hard at war, they sue so fast for peace, which by my advice they ne're shall have, unless they leave the Realm. Come noble Gloster, let's attend the King, it lies sir in your Son to do me pleasure, and save the charges of a Wedding Dinner, If you'l make haste to end your Love affairs, One cost may give discharge to both my cares.

(Exit DONOBERT, GLOSTER)

EDWIN: I'le do my best.

CADOR: Now Toclio, what stirring news at Court?

TOCLIO: Oh my Lord, the Court's all fill'd with rumor, the City with news, and the Country with wonder, and all the bells i'th' Kingdom must proclaim it, we have a new Holyday a coming.

CONSTANTIA: A holy-day! for whom? for thee?

TOCLIO: Me, Madam! 'sfoot I'de be loath that any man should make a holy-day for me yet: In brief 'tis thus, there's here arriv'd at Court, sent by the Earl of Chester to the King, a man of rare esteem for holyness, a reverent Hermit, that by miracle not onely saved our army, but without aid of man o'rethrew the pagan Host, and with such wonder sir, as might confirm a Kingdom to his faith.

EDWIN: This is strange news indeed, where is he?

TOCLIO: In conference with the King that much respects him.

MODESTIA: Trust me, I long to see him.

TOCLIO: Faith you will finde no great pleasure in him, for ought that I can see Lady, they say he is half a Prophet too, would he could tell me any news of the lost Prince, there's twenty Talents offer'd to him that finds him.

CADOR: Such news was breeding in the morning.

TOCLIO: And now it has birth and life sir, if fortune bless me I'le once more search those woods where then we lost him, I know not yet what fate may follow me.

(Exit TOCLIO)

CADOR: Fortune go with you sir, come fair Mistriss, your sister and Lord Edwin are in game, and all their wits at stake to win the Set.

CONSTANTIA: My sister has the hand yet, we had best leave them, She will be out anon as well as I, He wants but cunning to put in a Dye.

(Exit CADOR, CONSTANTIA)

EDWIN: You are a cunning gamester, Madam.

MODESTIA: It is a desperate Game indeed this Marriage, where there's no winning without loss to either.

EDWIN: Why, what but your perfection noble Lady, can bar the worthiness of this my suit? if so you please I count my happiness, from difficult obtaining, you shall see my duty and observance.

MODESTIA: There shall be place to neither, noble sir, I do beseech you let this mild Reply give answer to your suit, for here I vow if e're I change my Virgin name by you, it gains or looses.

EDWIN: My wishes have their crown.

MODESTIA: Let them confine you then, as to my promise, you give faith and credence?

EDWIN: In your command my willing absence speaks it.

(Exit EDWIN)

MODESTIA: Noble and vertuous: could I dream of Marriage, I should affect thee Edwin: oh my soul, here's something tells me that these best of creatures, these models of the world, weak man and woman, should have their souls, their making, life, and being, to some more excellent use: if what the sense calls pleasure were our ends, we might justly blame great natures wisdom, who rear'd a building of so much art and beauty to entertain a guest so far incertain, so imperfect: if onely speech distinguish us from beasts, who know no inequality of birth or place, but still to fly from goodness: oh, how base were life at such a rate! no, no, that power that gave to man his being, speech, and wisdom, gave it for thankfulness: To him alone that Made me thus, may I whence truly know, I'le pay to him, not man, the love I owe.

(Exit MODESTIA)

Scene 2: (Flourish Cornets. Enter AURELIUS, King of Brittain, DONOBERT, GLOSTER, CADOR, EDWIN, TOCLIO, OSWOLD, and Attendants.)

AURELIUS: No tiding of our brother yet? 'Tis strange, so ne're the Court, and in our own Land too, and yet no news of him: oh this loss tempers the sweetness of our happy conquests, with much untimely sorrow.

DONOBERT: Royal sir, his safety being unquestion'd, should to time leave the redress of sorrow, were he dead, or taken by the foe, our fatal loss had wanted no quick Herald to disclose it.

AURELIUS: That hope alone sustains me, nor will we do so ingrateful unto heaven to question what we fear, with what we enjoy. Is answer of our message yet return'd from that religious man, the holy Hermit, sent by the Earl of Chester to confirm us in that miraculous act? For 'twas no less, our Army being in rout, nay, quite o'rethrown, as Chester writes, even then this holy man arm'd with his cross and staff, went smiling on, and boldly fronts the foe; at fight of whom the Saxons stood amaz'd: for to their seeming, above the Hermit head appear'd such brightness, such clear and glorious beams as if our men march't all in fire, wherewith the Pagans fled, and by our troops were all to death pursu'd.

GLOSTER: 'Tis full of wonder sir.

AURELIUS: Oh Gloster, he's a jewel worth a Kingdom: where's Oswold with his answer?

OSWOLD: 'Tis here my Royal Lord.

AURELIUS: In writing, will he not sit with us?

OSWOLD: His Orizons perform'd, he bad me say he would attend with all submission.

AURELIUS: Proceed to councel then, and let some give order, the Embassadors being come, to take our answer, they have admittance. Oswold, Toclio, be it your charge: and now my Lords, observe the holy councel of this reveren'd Hermit: (reads) 'As you respect your safety, limit not that onely power that hath protected you, trust not an open enemy too far, He's yet a looser; and knows you have won, Mischiefs not ended, are but then begun.' Anselme the Hermit.

DONOBERT: Powerful and pithie, which my advice confirms, no man leaves physick when his sickness slakes, but doubles the receipts: the word of Peace seems fair to blood-shot eyes, but being appli'd with such a medicine as blinds all the fight, argues desire of Cure, but not of Art.

AURELIUS: You argue from defects, if both the name and the condition of the Peace be one, it is to be prefer'd, and in the offer made by the Saxon, I see nought repugnant.

GLOSTER: The time of Truce requir'd for thirty days, carries suspicion in it, since half that space will serve to strength their weakned Regiment.

CADOR: Who in less time will undertake to free our Country from them.

EDWIN: Leave that unto our fortune.

DONOBERT: Is not our bold, and hopeful General still Master of the field, their Legions faln, the rest intrencht for fear, half starv'd, and wounded, and shall we now give o're our fair advantage? force heaven, my Lord, the danger is far more, in trusting to their words, then to their weapons.

    (Enter OSWOLD)

OSWOLD: The Embassadors are come sir.

AURELIUS: Conduct them in, we are resolv'd my Lords, since policy fail'd in the beginning, it shall have no hand in the conclusion, that heavenly power that hath so well begun their fatal overthrow I know can end it, from which fair hope, my self will give them answer.

    (Flourish Cornets. Enter ARTESIA with the Saxon Lords)

DONOBERT: What's here, a woman Orator?

AURELIUS: Peace Donobert, speak, what are you Lady?

ARTESIA: The sister of the Saxon General, warlike Ostorius the East Anglese King, my name Artesia, who in terms of love brings peace and health to great Aurelius, wishing she may return as fair a present as she makes tender of.

AURELIUS: The fairest present e're mine eyes were blest with, command a chair there for this Saxon Beauty: sit Lady, we'l confer: your warlike brother sues for a peace, you say?

ARTESIA: With endless love unto your State and Person.

AURELIUS: He's sent a moving Orator believe me, what thinkst thou Donobert?

DONOBERT: Believe me sir, were I but yong agen this gilded pill might take my stomack quickly.

AURELIUS: True, thou art old, how soon we do forget our own defects. Fair damsel, oh my tongue turns Traitor, and will betray my heart, sister to our enemy: 's death her beauty mazes me, I cannot speak if I but look on her, what's that we did conclude?

DONOBERT: This, Royal Lord.

AURELIUS: Pish, thou canst not utter it; fair'st of creatures, tell the King your Brother that we in love, ha! and honour to our Country, command his armies to depart our Realm, but if you please fair soul Lord Donobert, deliver you our pleasure.

DONOBERT: I shall sir, Lady return, and certifie your brother.

AURELIUS: Thou art too blunt, and rude, return so soon, fie, let her stay, and send some messenger to certifie our pleasure.

DONOBERT: What meanes your Grace?

AURELIUS: To give her time of rest to her long Journey, we would not willingly be thought uncivil.

ARTESIA: Great King of Brittain, let it not seem strange to embrace the Princely Offers of a friend, Whose vertues with thine own, in fairest merit Both States in Peace and Love may now inherit.

AURELIUS: She speakes of Love agen, sure 'tis my fear, she knows I do not hate her.

ARTESIA: Be then thy self most great Aurelius, and let not envy, nor a deeper sin in these they Councellors, deprive thy goodness of that fair honor, we in seeking peace, give first to thee, who never use to sue but force our wishes; yet if this seem light, oh let my sex, though worthless your respect, take the report of thy humanity, Whose mild and vertuous life loud fame displays, As being o'recome by one so worthy praise.

AURELIUS: She has an Angels tongue, speak still.

DONOBERT: This flattery is gross sir, hear no more on't, Lady, these childish complements are needless, you have your answer, and believe it, Madam, his Grace, though young, doth wear within his breast too grave a Councellor to be seduc't by smoothing flattery, or oyly words.

ARTESIA: I come not sir, to wooe him.

DONOBERT: Twere folly if you should, you must not wed him, shame take thy tongue, being old and weak thy self, thou doat'st, and looking on thine own defects, speak'st what thoud'st wish in me, do I command the deeds of others, mine own act not free? Be pleas'd to smile or frown, we respect neither, My will and rule shall stand and fall together. Most fair Artesia, see the King descends to give thee welcome with these warlike Saxons, and now on equal terms both sires and grants, instead of Truce, let a perpetual League seal our united bloods in holy marriage, send the East Angles King this happy news, that thou with me hast made a League for ever, and added to his state a friend and brother: speak dearest Love, dare you confirm this Title?

ARTESIA: I were no woman to deny a good so high and noble to my fame and Country.

AURELIUS: Live then a Queen in Brittain.

GLOSTER: He meanes to marry her.

DONOBERT: Death! he shall marry the devil first, marry a Pagan, an Idolater.

CADOR: He has won her quickly.

EDWIN: She was woo'd afore she came sure, or came of purpose to conclude the Match.

AURELIUS: Who dare oppose our will? my Lord of Gloster, be you Embassador unto our Brother, the Brother of our Queen Artesia, tell him for such our entertainment looks him, our marriage adding to the happiness, Of our intended joys, mans good or ill, In this like waves agree, come double still,

    (Enter HERMIT)

Who's this, the Hermit? Welcome my happiness, our Countries hope, most reverent holy man, I wanted but thy blessing to make perfect the infinite sum of my felicity.

HERMIT: Alack sweet Prince, that happiness is yonder, Felicity and thou art far asunder, this world can never give it.

AURELIUS: Thou art deceiv'd, see here what I have found, Beauty, Alliance, Peace, and strength of Friends, all in this all exceeding excellence, the League's confirm'd.

HERMIT: With whom, dear Lord?

**AURELIUS AND ARTESIA**
I were no woman to deny a good so high and noble to my fame and Country.

AURELIUS: With the great Brother of this Beauteous woman, the Royal Saxon King.

HERMIT: Oh then I see, and fear thou art too near thy misery, what magick could so linck thee to this mischief by all the good that thou hast reapt by me, stand further from destruction.

AURELIUS: Speak as a man, and I shall hope to obey thee.

HERMIT: Idolaters get hence, fond King, let go, Thou hug'st thy ruine, and thy Countries woe.

DONOBERT: Well spoke old Father, to him, bait him soundly, now by heavens blest Lady, I can scarce keep patience.

1 SAX LORD: What devil is this?

2 SAX LORD: That cursed Christian, by whose hellish charmes our army was o'rethrown.

HERMIT: Why do you dally sir? oh tempt not heaven, warm not a serpent in your naked bosom, discharge them from your Court.

AURELIUS: Thou speak'st like madness, command the frozen shepherd to the shade, when he sits warm i'th'Sun, the fever sick to add more heat unto his burning pain, these may obey, 'tis less extremity then thou enjoynst to me: cast but thine eye upon this beauty, do it, I'le forgive thee, though jealousie in others findes no pardon, then say thou dost not love me, I shall then swear th'art immortal, and no earthly man, oh blame then my mortality, not me.

HERMIT: It is thy weakness brings thy misery, unhappy Prince.

AURELIUS: Be milder in thy doom.

HERMIT: 'Tis you that must indure heaven's doom, which faln, remember's just.

ARTESIA: Thou shalt not live to see it: how fares my Lord? If my poor presence breed dislike, great Prince, I am no such neglected soul, will seek to tie you to your word.

AURELIUS: My word dear Love, may my Religion, Crown, State, and Kingdom fail. When I fail thee, command Earl Chester to break up the camp, without disturbance to our Saxon friends, send every hour swift posts to hasten on the King her Brother, to conclude this League, this endless happy Peace of Love and Marriage, till when provide for Revels, and give charge that nought be wanting, which make our Triumphs Sportful and free to all, if such fair blood Ingender ill, man must not look for good.

(Exit all but HERMIT. Florish.
Enter MODESTIA reading in a book)

MODESTIA: How much the oft report of this blest Hermit, hath won on my desires; I must behold him, and sure this should be he, oh the worlds folly, proud earth and dust, how low a price bears goodness, all that should make man absolute, shines in him: much reverent Sir, may I without offence give interruption to your holy thoughts?

HERMIT: What would you Lady?

MODESTIA: That which till now ne're found a language in me, I am in love.

HERMIT: In Love, with what?

MODESTIA: With Vertue?

HERMIT: There's no blame in that.

MODESTIA: Nay sir, with you? With your Religious Life? Your Vertue, Goodness, if there be a name to express affection greater, that, that would I learn and utter: Reverent Sir, if there be any thing to bar my suit, be charitable and expose it, your prayers are the same Orizons, which I will number. Holy Sir, keep not instruction back from willingness, possess me of that knowledge leads you on to this humility, for well I know were greatness good, you would not live so low.

HERMIT: Are you a Virgin?

MODESTIA: Yes Sir?

HERMIT: Your name?

MODESTIA: Modestia?

HERMIT: Your name and vertues meet, a Modest Virgin, live ever in the sanctimonious way to Heaven and Happiness, there's goodness in you, I must instruct you further: come look up, behold yon firmament, there sits a power, whose foot-stool is this earth, oh learn this lesson, And practise it, he that will climb so high, Must leave no joy beneath, to move his eye.

(Exit HERMIT)

MODESTIA: I apprehend you sir, on Heaven I fix my love, Earth gives us grief, our joys are all above, For this was man in innocence naked born, To show us wealth hinders our sweet return.

(Exit MODESTIA)

# ACT II

*Scene 1*   (Enter CLOWN, and his sister great with childe)

CLOWN: Away, follow me no further, I am none of thy brother, what with Childe, great with Childe, and knows not whose the Father on't, I am asham'd to call thee Sister.

JOAN: Believe me Brother, he was a Gentleman.

CLOWN: Nay, I believe that, he gives arms, and legs too, and has made you the Herald to blaze 'em, but Joan, Joan, sister Joan, can you tell me his name that did it: how shall we call my Cousin, your bastard, when we have it?

JOAN: Alas, I know not the Gentlemans name Brother, I met him in these woods, the last great hunting, he was so kinde and proffer'd me so much, as I had not the heart to ask him more.

CLOWN: Not his name, why this showes your Country breeding now, had you been brought up i'th' City, you'd have got a Father first, and the childe afterwards: hast thou no markes to know him by.

JOAN: He had most rich Attire, a fair Hat and Feather, a gilt Sword, and most excellent Hangers.

CLOWN: Pox on his Hangers, would he had bin gelt for his labor.

JOAN: Had you but heard him swear you would have thought.

CLOWN: I as you did, swearing and lying goes together still, did his Oathes get you with Childe, we shall have a roaring Boy then yfaith, well sister, I must leave you.

JOAN: Dear Brother stay, help me to finde him out, I'le ask no further.

CLOWN: 'Sfoot who should I finde? who should I ask for?

JOAN: Alas I know not, he uses in these woods, and these are witness of his oathes and promise.

CLOWN: We are like to have a hot suit on't, when our best witness's but a knight 'ath'Post.

JOAN: Do but enquire this Forrest, I'le go with you, some happy fate may guide us till we meet him.

CLOWN: Meet him, and what name shall we have for him, when we meet him? 'Sfoot thou neither knowst him, nor canst tell what to

**THE CLOWN**
Away, follow me no further . . .

call him, was ever man tyr'd with such a business, to have a sister got with childe, and know not who did it, well, you shall see him, I'le do my best for you, Ile make Proclamation, if these Woods and Trees, as you say, will bear any witness, let them answer; Oh yes: If there be any man that wants a name, will come in for conscience sake, and acknowledge himself to be a Whore-Master, he shal have that laid to his charge in an hour, he shall not be rid on in an age, if he have Lands, he shall have an heir, if he have patience, he shall have a wife, if he have neither Lands nor patience, he shall have a whore, so ho boy, so ho, so, so.

(Within) PRINCE UTER: So, ho, by, so, ho, illo ho, illo ho.

CLOWN: Hark, hark sister, there's one hollows to us, what a wicked world's this, a man cannot so soon name a whore but a knave comes presently, and see where he is, stand close a while, sister.

(Enter PRINCE UTER)

PRINCE: How like a voice that Eccho spake, but oh my thoughts are lost for ever in amazement, could I but meet a man to tell her beauties, these trees would bend their tops to kiss the air, that from my lips should give her praises up.

CLOWN: He talk's of a woman, sister.

JOAN: This may be he, brother.

CLOWN: View him well, you see he has a fair Sword, but his Hanger's are faln.

PRINCE: Here did I see her first, here view her beauty, oh had I known her name, I had been happy.

CLOWN: Sister this is he sure, he knows not thy name neither a couple of wise fools yfaith, to get children and know not one another.

PRINCE: You weeping leaves, upon whose tender cheeks doth stand a flood of tears at my complaint, and heard my vows and oathes.

CLOWN: Law, Law, he has been a great swearer too, 'tis he sister.

PRINCE: For having overtook her, as I have seen a forward blood-hound, strip the swifter of the cry ready to seize his wished hopes, upon the sudden view struck with astonishment at his arriv'd prey, instead of seizure stands at fearful bay, Or Like to Marius soldiers, who o'retook The eye sight killing Gorgon at one look, Made everlasting stand: so fear'd my power Whose cloud aspir'd the Sun, dissolv'd a shower:

Pigmalion, then I tasted thy sad fate, whose Ivory picture, and my fair were one, our dotage past imagination, I saw and felt desire.

CLOWN: Pox a your fingering, did he feel sister?

PRINCE: But enjoy'd not, oh fate, thou hadst thy days and nights to feed,
Or calm affection, one poor fight was all, Converts my pleasure to perpetual thrall, Imbracing shine, thou lostest breath and desire, So I relating mine, will here expire, For here I vow to you mournful plants, Who were the first made happy by her fame, Never to part hence, till I know her name.

CLOWN: Give me thy hand sister, The Childe has found his Father, this is he sure, as I am a man, had I been a woman these kinde words would have won me, I should have had a great belly too that's certain, well, I'le speak to him: most honest and fleshly minded Gentleman, give me your hand sir.

PRINCE: Ha, what art thou, that thus rude and boldly, darest take notice of a wretch so much ally'd to misery as I am?

CLOWN: Nay, Sir, for our aliance, I shall be found to be a poor brother in Law of your worships, the Gentlewoman you spake on, is my sister, you see what a clew she spreads, her name is Joan Go-too't, I am her elder, but she has been at it before me: 'tis a womans fault, pox a this bashfulness, come forward Jug, prethee speak to him.

PRINCE: Have you e're seen me Lady?

CLOWN: Seen ye, ha, ha, It seems she has felt you too, here's a yong Go-too't a coming sir, she is my sister, we all love to Go-too't, as well as your worship, she's a Maid yet, but you may make her a wife, when you please sir.

PRINCE: I am amaz'd with wonder: Tell me woman, what sin have you committed worthy this?

JOAN: Do you not know me sir?

PRINCE: Know thee! as I do thunder, hell, and mischief, witch, stallion, hag.

CLOWN: I see he will marry her, he speaks so like a husband.

PRINCE: Death, I will cut their tongues out for this blasphemy, strumpet, villain, where have you ever seen me?

CLOWN: Speak for your self with a pox to ye.

*The Childe hath found his Father*

PRINCE: Slaves, Ile make you curse your selves for this temptation.

JOAN: Oh sir, if ever you did speak to me, it was in smoother phrase, in fairer language.

PRINCE: Lightning consume me, if I ever saw thee, my rage o'reflowes my blood, all patience flies me.

   (Beats her)

CLOWN: Hold I beseech you sir, I have nothing to say to you.

JOAN: Help, help, murder, murder.

   (Enter TOCLIO, and OSWOLD)

TOCLIO: Make haste Sir, this way the sound came, it was a wood.

OSWOLD: See where she is, and the Prince, the price of all our wishes.

CLOWN: The Prince say ye, ha's made a poor Subject of me I am sure.

TOCLIO: Sweet Prince, noble Uter, speak, how fare you sir?

OSWOLD: Dear sir, recal your self, your fearful absence hath won too much already on the grief of our sad King, from whom our laboring search hath had this fair success in meeting you.

TOCLIO: His silence, and his looks argue distraction.

CLOWN: Nay, he's mad sure, he will not acknowledge my sister, nor the childe neither.

OSWOLD: Let us entreat your Grace along with us, your sight will bring new life, to the King your Brother.

TOCLIO: Will you go sir?

PRINCE: Yes, any whether, guide me, all's hell I see, Man may change air, but not his misery.

   (Exit PRINCE, TOCLIO)

JOAN: Lend me one word with you, sir.

CLOWN: Well said sister, he has a Feather, and fair Hangers too, this may be he.

OSWOLD: What would you fair one.

CLOWN: Sure I have seen you in these woods e're this?

OSWOLD: Trust me never, I never saw this place, till at this time my friend conducted me.

JOAN: The more's my sorrow then.

OSWOLD: Would I could comfort you: I am a Bachelor, but it seems you have a husband, you have been fouly o'reshot else.

CLOWN: A womans fault, we are all subject to go to't, sir.

    (Enter TOCLIO)

TOCLIO: Oswold away, the Prince will not stir a foot without you.

OSWOLD: I am coming, farewel woman.

TOCLIO: Prithee make haste.

JOAN: Good sir, but one word with you e're you leave us.

TOCLIO: With me fair soul?

CLOWN: Shee'l have a fling at him too, the Childe must have a Father.

JOAN: Have you ne'er seen me sir?

TOCLIO: Seen thee, 'Sfoot I have seen many fair faces in my time, prithee look up, and do not weep so, sure pretty wanton, I have seen this face before.

JOAN: It is enough, though you ne're see me more.

    (Sinks down)

TOCLIO: 'Sfoot she's faln, this place is inchanted sure, look to the woman fellow.

                                           (Exit TOCLIO)

CLOWN: Oh she's dead! she's dead, as you are a man stay and help, sir: Joan, Joan, sister Joan, why Joan Go-too't I say, will you cast away your self, and your childe, and me too, what do you mean, sister?

JOAN: Oh give me pardon sir, 'twas too much joy opprest my loving thoughts, I know you were too noble to deny me, ha! Where is he?

CLOWN: Who, the Gentleman? he's gone sister.

JOAN: Oh! I am undone then, run, tell him I did but faint for joy, dear brother haste, why dost thou stay? oh never cease, till he give answer to thee.

CLOWN: He: which he? what do you call him tro?

JOAN: Unnatural brother, shew me the path he took, why dost thou dally? speak, oh which way went he?

CLOWN: This way, that way, through the bushes there.

JOAN: Were it through fire, the Journey's easie, winged with sweet desire.

                                           (Exit JOAN)

CLOWN: Hey day, there's some hope of this yet, Ile follow her for kindreds sake, if she miss of her purpose now, she'l challenge all she findes I see, for if ever we meet with a two leg'd creature in the whole Kingdom, the Childe shall have a Father that's certain.

(Exit CLOWN)

> Scene 2:  Loud Music. Enter two with the Sword and Mace, CADOR, EDWIN, two Bishops, AURELIUS, OSTORIUS leading ARTESIA Crown'd, CONSTANTIA, MODESTIA, OCTA, PROXIMUS a Magician, DONOBERT, GLOSTER, OSWOLD, TOCLIO, all pass over the stage. Manet DONOBERT, GLOSTER, EDWIN, CADOR.)

DONOBERT: Come Gloster, I do not like this hasty Marriage.

GLOSTER: She was quickly wooed and won, not six days since arrived an enemy to sue for Peace, and now crown'd Queen of Brittain, this is strange.

DONOBERT: Her brother too made as quick speed in coming, leaving his Saxons, and his starved Troops, to take the advantage whilst 'twas offer'd, fore heaven I fear the King's too credulous, our Army is discharg'd too.

GLOSTER: Yes, and our General commanded home, Son Edwin have you seen him since?

EDWIN: He's come to Court, but will not view the presence, nor speak unto the King, he's so discontent at this so strange alliance with the Saxon, as nothing can perswade his patience.

CADOR: You know his humor will indure no check, no, if the King oppose it, all crosses feeds both his spleen, and his impatience, those affections are in him like powder, apt to inflame with every little spark, and blow up all his reason.

GLOSTER: Edol of Chester is a noble Soldier.

DONOBERT: So is he by the Rood, ever most faithful to the King and Kingdom, how e're his passions guide him.

> (Enter EDOLL with Captains)

CADOR: See where he comes, my Lord.

OMNES: Welcome to Court, brave Earl.

EDOL: Do not deceive me by your flatteries: Is not the Saxon here? the League confirm'd? the Marriage ratifi'd? the Court divided with Pagan Infidels? the least part Christians, at least in their Commands? Oh the gods! it is a thought that takes away my sleep, and dulls my senses so I scarcely know you: Prepare my horses, Ile away to Chester.

CAPTAINS: What shall we do with our Companies, my Lord?

EDOL: Keep them at home to increase Cuckolds, and get some Cases for your Captainships, smooth up your brows, the wars has spoil'd your faces, and few will now regard you.

DONOBERT: Preserve your patience, Sir.

EDOL: Preserve your Honors, Lords, your Countries Safety, your Lives, and Lands from strangers; what black devil could so bewitch the King, so to discharge a Royal Army in the height of conquest? nay, even already made victorious, to give such credit to an enemy, a starved foe, a stragling fugitive, beaten beneath our feet, so love dejected, so servile, and so base, as hope of life had won them all, to leave the Land for ever?

DONOBERT: It was the Kings will.

EDOL: It was your want of wisdom, that should have laid before his tender youth, the dangers of a State, where forain Powers bandy for Soveraignty with Lawful Kings, who being setled once, to assure themselves, will never fail to seek the blood and life of all competitors.

DONOBERT: Your words sound well my Lord, and point at safety, both for the Realm and us, but why did you within whose power it lay, as General, with full Commission to dispose the war, lend ear to parly with the weakned foe?

EDOL: Oh the good Gods!

CADOR: And on that parly came this Embassie.

EDOL: You will hear me.

EDWIN: Your letters did declare it to the King, both of the Peace, and all Conditions brought by this Saxon Lady, whose fond love has thus bewitched him.

EDOL: I will curse you all as black as hell, unless you hear me, your gross mistake would make wisdom herself run madding through the streets, and quarrel with her shadow, death! why kill'd ye not that woman?

DONOBERT, GLOSTER: Oh my Lord.

EDOL: The great devil take me quick, had I been by and all the women of the world were barren, she should have died e're he had married her on these conditions.

CADOR: It is not reason that directs you thus.

EDOL: Then have I none, for all I have directs me, never was man so palpably abus'd, so basely marted, bought and sold to scorn, my

Honor, Fame, and hopeful Victories, the loss of Time, Expences, Blood and Fortunes, all vanisht into nothing.

EDWIN: This rage is vain my Lord, what the King does, nor they, nor you can help.

EDOL: My Sword must fail me then.

CADOR: 'Gainst whom will you expose it?

EDOL: What's that to you, 'gainst all the devils in hell to guard my country.

EDWIN: These are airy words.

EDOL: Sir, you tread too hard upon my patience.

EDWIN: I speak the duty of a Subjects faith, and say again had you been here in presence, What the King did, you had not dar'd to cross it,

EDOL: I will trample on his Life and Soul that says it.

CADOR: My Lord.

EDWIN: Come, come,

EDOL: Now before heaven.

CADOR: Dear sir.

EDOL: Not dare? thou liest beneath thy lungs.

GLOSTER: No more son Edwin.

EDWIN: I have done sir, I take my leave.

EDOL: But thou shall not, you shall take no leave of me Sir.

DONOBERT: For wisdoms sake my Lord.

EDOL: I'le leave him and you, and all of you, the Court and King, and let my Sword, and friends, shuffle for Edols safety: stay you here, and hug the Saxons, till they cut your throats, or bring the Land to servile slavery, such yokes of basements, Chester must not suffer, Go, and repent betimes these foul misdeeds, For in this League, all our whole Kingdom bleeds, which Ile prevent, or perish.

GLOSTER: See how his rage transports him!

(Exit EDOL, Captain)

CADOR: These passions set apart, a braver soldier breathes not i'th' world this day.

DONOBERT: I wish his own worth do not court his ruine. The King must Rule, and we must learn to obey, True vertue still directs the noble way.

*Scene 3* (Loud Musick. Enter AURELIUS, ARTESIA, OSTORIUS, OCTA, PROXIMUS, TOCLIO, OSWOLD, HERMIT)

AURELIUS: Why is the Court so dull? me thinks each room, and angle of our Palace should appear stuck full of objects fit for mirth and triumphs, to show our high content. Oswold fill wine, must we begin the Revels? be it so then, reach me the cup: Ile now begin a Health to our lov'd Queen, the bright Artesia, the Royal Saxon King, our warlike brother, go and command all the whole Court to pledge it, fill to the Hermit there, most reverent Anselme, wee'l do thee Honor first, to pledge my Queen.

HERMIT: I drink no healths great King, and if I did, I would be loath to part with health, to those that have no power to give it back again.

AURELIUS: Mistake not, it is the argument of Love and Duty to our Queen and us.

ARTESIA: But he owes none it seems.

HERMIT: I do to vertue Madam, temperate minds covets that health to drink, which nature gives in every spring to man, he that doth hold His body, but a Tenement at will Bestows no cost, but to repair what's ill, Yet if your healths or heat of Wine, fair Princes, Could this old frame, or these cras'd limbes restore, Or keep out death, or sickness, then fill more, I'le make fresh way for appetite, if no, On such a prodigal who would wealth bestow?

OSTORIUS: He speaks not like a guest to grace a wedding.

(Enter TOCLIO)

ARTESIA: No sir, but like an envious imposter.

OCTA: A Christian slave, a Cinick.

OSTORIUS: What vertue could decline your Kingly spirit, to such respect of him whose magick spells met with your vanquisht Troops, and turn'd your Arms to that necessity of fight, which the dispair of any hope to stand but by his charms, had been defeated in a bloody conquest?

OCTA: 'Twas magick, hell-bred magick did it sir, and that's a course my Lord, which we esteem in all our Saxon wars, unto the last and lowest ebbe of servile treachery.

AURELIUS: Sure you are deceive'd, it was the hand of heaven, that in his vertue gave us victory, is there a power in man that can strike fear thorough a general camp, or create spirits, in recreant bosoms above present sense?

OSTORIUS: To blind the sense there may with apparition of well arm'd troops within themselves are air, form'd into humane shapes, and such that day were by that Sorcerer rais'd to cross our fortunes.

AURELIUS: There is a law tells us, that words want force to make deeds void, examples must be shown by instances alike, e're I believe it.

OSTORIUS: 'Tis easily perform'd, believe me sir, propose your own desires, and give but way to what our Magick here shall straight perform, and then let his or our deserts be censur'd.

AURELIUS: We could not with a greater happiness, then what this satisfaction brings with it, let him proceed, fair brother.

OSTORIUS: He shall sir, come learned Proximus, this task be thine, let thy great charms confound the opinion this Christian by his spells hath falsly won.

PROXIMUS: Great King, propound your wishes then, what persons, of what State, what numbers, or how arm'd, please your own thoughts, they shall appear before you.

AURELIUS: Strange art! what thinkst thou reverent Hermit?

HERMIT: Let him go on sir.

AURELIUS: Wilt thou behold his cunning?

HERMIT: Right gladly sir, it will be my joy to tell, That I was here to laugh at him and hell.

AURELIUS: I like thy confidence.

ARTESIA: His sawcy impudence, proceed to'th' trial.

PROXIMUS: Speak your desires my Lord, and be it place't in any angle underneath the Moon, the center of the Earth, the Sea, the Air, the region of the fire, nay hell itself, and I'le present it.

AURELIUS: Wee'l have no sight so fearful, onely this, if all thy art can reach it, show me here the two great Champions of the Trojan War, Achilles and Brave Hector, our great Ancestor, both in the warlike habits, Armor, Shields, and Weapons then in use for fight.

PROXIMUS: 'Tis done, my Lord, command a halt and silence, as each man will respect his life or danger, Armel, Plesgeth!

(Enter SPIRITS)

SPIRIT: Quid vis?

**PROXIMUS SUMMONS THE SHADES OF HECTOR AND ACHILLES**
The Apparition comes, on our displeasure let all keep place and silence.

PROXIMUS: Attend me.

AURELIUS: The Apparition comes, on our displeasure let all keep place and silence.

> (Within Drums beat Marches.
> Enter PROXIMUS bringing in HECTOR attir'd and armed after the Trojan manner, with Target, Sword, and Battle-axe, a trumpet before him and a spirit in flame colours with a Torch, at the other door ACHILLES with his spear and Falchon, a Trumpet and a Spirit in black before him. Trumpets sound alarm, and they manage their weapons to begin the Fight: and after some charges, the HERMIT steps between them, at which seeming, amaz'd the spirits, and tremble. Thunder within)

PROXIMUS: What means this stay, bright Armel, Plesgeth? why fear you and fall back? renew the Alarms, and enforce the Combat, or hell or darkness circles you for ever.

ARMEL: We dare not.

PROXIMUS: Ha!

PLESGETH: Our charms are all dissolv'd, Armel away, 'Tis worse than hell to us, whilst here we stay.

(Exit all)

HERMIT: What! at a Non-plus sir? command them back for shame.

PROXIMUS: What power o're-aws my Spells! return you Hellhounds, Armel, Plesgeth, double damnation seize you, by all the Infernal powers, the prince of devils in this Hermits habit, what else could force my spirits quake or tremble thus?

HERMIT: Weak argument to hide your want of skill: does the devil fear the devil, or war with hell? they have not been acquainted long it seems. Know misbelieving Pagan, even that power That overthrew your Forces, still lets you see, He onely can controul both hell and thee.

PROXIMUS: Disgrace and mischief, Ile enforce new charms, new spells, and spirits rais'd from the low Abyss of hells unbottom'd depths.

AURELIUS: We have enough sir, give o're your charms, wee'l finde some other time to praise your Art. I dare not but acknowledge that heavenly Power my heart stands witness to: be not dismaid my Lords, at this disaster, nor thou my fairest Queen: we'l change the Scene to some more pleasing sports, Lead to your Chamber,

## The Birth of Merlin

How'ere in this thy pleasures finde a cross, Our joy's too fixed here to suffer loss.

TOCLIO: Which I shall adde to sir, with news I bring: The Prince your Brother, lives.

AURELIUS: Ha!

TOCLIO: And comes to grace this high and heaven-knit Marriage.

AURELIUS: Why dost thou flatter me, to make me think such happiness attends me?

(Enter Prince UTER and OSWOLD)

TOCLIO: His presence speaks my truth, sir.

DONOBERT: Force me, 'tis he: look Gloster.

GLOSTER: A blessing beyond hope, sir.

AURELIUS: Ha! 'tis he: welcome my second Comfort. Artesia, Dearest Love, it is my Brother, my Princely Brother, all my Kingdoms hope, oh give him welcome, as thou lov'st my health.

ARTESIA: You have so free a welcome sir, from me, as this your presence has such power I swear o're me a stranger, that I must forget my Countrey, Name and Friends, and count this place my Joy and Birth right.

PRINCE: 'Tis she! 'tis I swear! oh ye good gods, 'tis she! that face within those woods where first I saw her, captivated my senses, and thus many moneths bar'd me from all society of men: how came she to this place, brother Aurelius? Speak that Angels name, her heaven-blest name, oh speak it quickly Sir.

AURELIUS: It is Artesia, the Royal Saxon Princess.

PRINCE: A woman, and a Deity: no feigned shape, to mock the reason of admiring sense, on whom a hope as low as mine may live, love, and enjoy, dear Brother, may it not?

AURELIUS: She is all the Good, or Vertue thou canst name, my Wife, my Queen.

PRINCE: Ha! your wife!

ARTESIA: Which you shall finde sir, if that time and fortune may make my love but worthy of your tryal.

PRINCE: Oh!

AURELIUS: What troubles you, dear Brother? Why with so strange and fixt an eye dost thou behold my Joys?

ARTESIA: You are not well, sir.

PRINCE: Yes, yes, oh you immortal powers, why has poor man so many entrances for sorrow to creep in at, when our sense is much too weak to hold his happiness? Oh say I was born deaf: and let your silence confirm in me the knowing my defect, at least be charitable to conceal my sin, for hearing is no less in me, dear Brother.

AURELIUS: No more, I see thou art a Rival in the Joys of my high Bliss. Come my Artesia, The Day's most prais'd when 'tis ecclipst by Night, Great Good must have as great Ill opposite.

PRINCE: Stay, hear but a word; yet now I think on't, This is your Wedding-night, and were it mine, I should be angry with least loss of time.

ARTESIA: Envy speaks no such words, has no such looks.

PRINCE: Sweet rest unto you both.

AURELIUS: Lights to our Nuptial Chamber.

ARTESIA: Could you speak so, I would not fear how much my grief did grow.

AURELIUS: Lights to our Chamber, on, on, set on.

*(Exeunt. Manet PRINCE)*

PRINCE: Could you speak so, I would not fear how much my griefs did grow. Those were her very words, sure I am waking, she wrung me by the hand, and spake them to me with a most passionate affection, perhaps she loves, and now repents her choice, in marriage with my brother; oh fond man, how darest thou trust thy Traitors thoughts, thus to betray thy self? 'twas but a waking dream wherein thou madest thy wishes speak, not her, in which they foolish hopes strives to prolong A wretched being, so sickly children play With health lov'd toys, which for a time delay, But do not cure the fit: be then a man, Meet that destruction which thou canst not flie From, not to live, make it thy best to die, And call her now, whom thou didst hope to wed, Thy brothers wife, thou art too ne're a kin, And such an act above all name's a sin Not to be blotted out, heaven pardon me, She's banisht from my bosom now for ever, To lowest ebbes, men justly hope a flood, When vice grows barren, all desires are good.

(Enter Waiting Gentlewoman with a Jewel)

GENTLEWOMAN: The noble Prince, I take it sir.

PRINCE: You speak me what I should be, Lady.

GENTLEWOMAN: Know by that name sir, Queen Artesia greets you.

PRINCE: Alas good vertue, how is she mistaken.

GENTLEWOMAN: Commending her affection in this Jewel, sir.

PRINCE: She binds my service to her: ha! a Jewel 'tis a fair one trust me, and methinks it much resembles something I have seen with her.

GENTLEWOMAN: It is an artificial crab, Sir.

PRINCE: A creature that goes backward!

GENTLEWOMAN: True, from the way it looks.

PRINCE: There is no moral in it aludes to her self?

GENTLEWOMAN: 'Tis your construction gives you that sir, she's a woman.

PRINCE: And like this, may use her legs, and eyes two several ways.

GENTLEWOMAN: Just like the Sea-crab, which on the Mussel prayes, whilst he bills at a stone.

PRINCE: Pretty in troth, prithee tell me, art thou honest?

GENTLEWOMAN: I hope I seem no other, sir.

PRINCE: And those that seem so, are sometimes bad enough.

GENTLEWOMAN: If they will accuse themselves for want of witness, let them, I am not so foolish.

PRINCE: I see th'art wife, come speak me truly, what is the greatest sin?

GENTLEWOMAN: That which man never acted, what has been done Is as the least, common to all as one.

PRINCE: Dost think thy Lady is of thy opinion?

GENTLEWOMAN: She's a bad Scholar else, I have brought her up, and she dares owe me still.

PRINCE: I, 'tis a fault in greatness, they dare owe many e're they pay one, but darest thou expose thy scholar to my examining?

GENTLEWOMAN: Yes in good troth sir, and pray put her to't too, 'tis a hard lesson if she answer it not.

PRINCE: Thou know'st the hardest.

GENTLEWOMAN: As far as a woman may, sir.

PRINCE: I commend thy plainness, when wilt thou bring me to thy Lady?

GENTLEWOMAN: Next opportunity I attend you, sir.

PRINCE: Thanks, take this, and commend me to her.

GENTLEWOMAN: Think of your Sea-crab sir, I pray.

(Exit GENTLEWOMAN)

PRINCE: Oh by any means, Lady, what should all this tend to? if it be Love or Lust that thus incites her, the sin is horrid and incestuous, if to betray my life, what hopes she by it? Yes, it may be a practice 'twixt themselves, to expel the Brittains and ensure the State through our destructions, all this may be valid with a deeper reach in villany, then all my thoughts can guess at; however I will confer with her, and if I finde Lust hath given Life to Envy in her minde, I may prevent the danger, so men wise
By the same step by which they fell, may rise.
Vices are Vertues, if so thought and seen,
And Trees with foulest roots, branch soonest green.

(Exit PRINCE)

# ACT III.

*Scene 1* (Enter CLOWN and his Sister)

CLOWN: Come sister, thou that art all fool, all mad-woman.

JOAN: Prithee have patience, we are now at Court.

CLOWN: At Court! ha, ha, that proves they madness, was there ever any woman in thy taking travel'd to Court for a husband? 'slid, 'tis enough for them to get children, and the City to keep 'em, and the Countrey to finde Nurses: everything must be done in his due place, sister.

JOAN: Be but content a while, for sure I know this Journey will be happy. Oh dear brother, this night my sweet Friend came to comfort me, I saw him, and embrac't him in my arms.

CLOWN: Why did you not hold him, and call me to help you?

JOAN: Alas, I thought I had been with him still, but when I wak't!

CLOWN: Ah pox of all Loger-heads, then you were but in a Dream all this while, and we may still go look him: Well, since we are come to Court, cast your Cats eyes about you, and either finde him out you dreamt on, or some other, for Ile trouble my self no further.

(Enter DONOBERT, CADOR, EDWIN AND TOCLIO)

CLOWN: See, see, here comes more Courtiers, look about you, come, pray view 'em all well; the old man has none of the marks about him, the other have both Swords and Feathers: what thinkest thou of that tall yong Gentleman?

JOAN: He much resembles him, but sure my friend, brother, was not so high of stature.

CLOWN: Oh beast, wast thou got a childe with a short thing too?

DONOBERT: Come, come, Ile hear no more on't: Go Lord Edwin, tell her this day her sister shall be married to Cador Earl of Cornwal, so shall she to thee brave Edwin, if she'l have my Blessing.

EDWIN: She is addicted to a single Life, she will not hear of Marriage.

DONOBERT: Tush, fear it not: go you from me to her, use your best skill my Lord, and if you fail, I have a trick shall do it: haste about it.

EDWIN: Sir, I am gone, my hope is in your help more then my own.

DONOBERT: And worthy Toclio, to your care I must commend this business, for Lights and Musick, and what else is needful.

TOCLIO: I shall my Lord.

*The Childe hath found his Father*

CLOWN: We would intreat a word sir, come forward sister.

(Exit DONOBERT, TOCLIO, CADOR)

EDWIN: What lackst thou fellow?

CLOWN: I lack a father for a childe, sir.

EDWIN: How! a God-father?

CLOWN: No sir, we mean the own father: it may be you sir, for any thing we know, I think the childe is like you.

EDWIN: Like me! prithee where is it?

CLOWN: Nay, 'tis not born yet sir, 'tis forth coming you see, the childe must have a father; what do you think of my sister?

EDWIN: Why I think if she ne're had husband she's a whore and thou a fool, farewell.

(Exit EDWIN)

CLOWN: I thank you sir: well, pull up thy heart sister, if there be any Law i'th Court this fellow shall father it, 'cause he uses me so scurvily. There's a great Wedding towards they say, we'l amongst them for a husband for thee.

(Enter SIR NICODEMUS with a Letter)

If we miss there, Ile have another bout with him that abus'd me: See! look, there comes another Hat and Feather, this should be a close Letcher, he's reading of a Love-letter.

NICODEMUS: Earl Cador's Marriage, and a Masque to grace it, so, so. This night shall make me famous for Presentments. How now, what are you?

CLOWN: A couple of Great Brittains, you may see by our bellies, sir.

NICODEMUS: And what of this sir?

CLOWN: Why thus the matter stands sir: There's one of your Courtiers Hunting Nags has made a Gap through another mans Inclosure. Now sir, here's the question, who should be at charge of a Fur-bush to stop it?

NICODEMUS: Ha, ha, this is out of my element: the Law must end it.

CLOWN: Your Worship says well; for surely I think some Lawyer had a hand in the business, we have such a troublesom Issue.

NICODEMUS: But what's thy business with me now?

CLOWN: Nay sir, the business is done already, you may see by my sisters belly.

NICODEMUS: Oh, now I finde thee, this Gentlewoman it seems has been humbled.

CLOWN: As low as the ground would give her leave sir, and your Worship knows this: though there be many fathers without children, yet to have a childe without a father, were most unnatural.

NICODEMUS: That's true i'faith, I never heard of a childe yet that e're begot his father.

CLOWN: Why true, you say wisely sir.

NICODEMUS: And therefore I conclude, that he that got the childe, is without all question the father of it.

CLOWN: I, now you come to the matter sir: and our suit is to your Worship for the discovery of this father.

NICODEMUS: Why, lives he in the Court here?

JOAN: Yes sir, and I desire but Marriage.

NICODEMUS: And does the knave refuse it? Come, come, be merry wench, he shall marry thee, and keep the childe too, if my Knighthood can do anything; I am bound by mine Orders to help distressed Ladies, and can there be a greater injury to a woman with childe, than to lack a father for't? I am asham'd of your simpleness: Come, come, give me a Courtiers Fee for my pains, and Ile be thy Advocate my self, and justice shall be found, nay Ile sue the Law for it; but give me my Fee first.

CLOWN: If all the money I have i'th world will do it, you shall have it sir.

NICODEMUS: An Angel does it.

CLOWN: Nay there's two, for your better eye sight sir.

NICODEMUS: Why well said: give me thy hand wench, Ile teach thee a trick for all this, shall get a father for thy childe presently, and this it is, mark now: You meet a man, as you meet me now, thou claimest Marriage of me, and layest the childe to my charge, I deny it: push, that's nothing, hold thy Claim fast, thy words carries it, and no Law can withstand it.

CLOWN: Ist possible?

NICODEMUS: Past all opposition, her own word carries it, let her challenge any man, the childe shall call him father, there's a trick for your money now.

CLOWN: Troth Sir, we thank you, we'l make use of your trick, and go no further to seek the childe a Father, for we challenge you Sir: sister lay it to him, he shall marry thee, I shall have a worshipful old man to my brother.

NICODEMUS: Ha, ha, I like thy pleasantness.

JOAN: Nay indeed Sir, I do challenge you.

CLOWN: You think we jest sir.

NICODEMUS: I by my troth do I, I like thy wit yfaith, thou shalt live at Court with me, didst never here of Nicodemus Nothing? I am the man.

CLOWN: Nothing, 'slid we are out agen, thou wast never got with childe with nothing sure.

JOAN: I know not what to say.

NICODEMUS: Never grieve wench, show me the man and process shall fly out.

CLOWN: 'Tis enough for us to finde the children, we look that you should finde the Father, and therefore either do us justice, or we'l stand to our first challenge.

NICODEMUS: Would you have justice without an Adversary, unless you can show me the man, I can do you no good in it.

CLOWN: Why then I hope you'l do us no harm sir, you'l restore my money.

NICODEMUS: What, my Fee? marry Law forbid it, finde out the party, and you shall have justice, your fault clos'd up, and all shall be amended, the Childe his Father, and the Law defended.

(Exit SIR NICODEMUS)

CLOWN: Well, he has deserv'd his Fee indeed, for he has brought our suit to a quick end, I promise you, and yet the Childe has never a Father; nor we have no more money to seek after him, a shame of all lecherous placcats, now you look like a Cat had newly kitten'd, what will you do now tro? Follow me no further, lest I beat your brains out.

JOAN: Impose upon me any punishment, rather than leave me now.

CLOWN: Well, I think I am bewitcht with thee; I cannot finde in my heart to forsake her. There was never sister would have abus'd a poor brother as thou hast done, I am even pin'd away with fretting, there's nothing but flesh and bones about me, well and I had my money agen, it were some comfort, hark sister,

(Thunder)
does it not thunder?

JOAN: Oh yes, most fearfully, what shall we do brother?

CLOWN: Marry e'ene get some shelter e're the storm catch us: away, let's away I prithee.

> (Enter the DEVIL in mans habit, richly attired, his feet and his head horrid)

JOAN: Ha, 'tis he, stay brother, dear brother stay.

CLOWN: What's the matter now?

JOAN: My love, my friend is come, yonder he goes.

CLOWN: Where, where, show me where, I'le stop him if the devil be not in him.

JOAN: Look there, look yonder, oh dear friend, pity my distress, for heaven and goodness do but speak to me.

DEVIL: She calls me, and yet drives me headlong from her,
Poor mortal, thou and I are much uneven,
Thou must not speak of goodness nor of heaven,
If I confer with thee: but be of comfort,
Whilst men do breath, and Brittains name be known,
The fatal fruit thou bear'st within thy womb,
Shall here be famous till the day of doom.

CLOWN: 'Slid who's that talks so? I can see no body.

JOAN: Then art thou blind, or mad, see where he goes, and beckons me to come, oh lead me forth, I'le follow thee in spight of fear or death.

(Exit JOAN)

CLOWN: Oh brave, she'l run to the devil for a husband, she's stark mad sure, and talks to a shaddow, for I could see no substance: well, I'le after her, the childe was got by chance, and the father must be found at all adventure.

(Exit CLOWN)

Scene 2    (Enter HERMIT, MODESTIA and EDWIN)

MODESTIA: Oh reverent sir, by you my heart hath reacht at the large hopes of holy Piety, and for this I craved your company,
Here in your fight religiously to vow,
My chaste thoughts up to heaven, and make you now the witness of my faith.

HERMIT: Angels assist thy hopes.

EDWIN: What means my Love? thou art my promis'd wife.

MODESTIA: To part with willingly what friends and life can make no good assurance of.

EDWIN: Oh finde remorse, fair soul, to love and merit, and yet recant thy vow.

MODESTIA: Never: this world and I are parted now for ever.

HERMIT: To finde the way to bliss, oh happy woman,
Th'ast learn'd the hardest Lesson well I see,
Now show thy fortitude and constancy,
Let these thy friends thy sad departure weep,
Thou shalt but loose the wealth thou could'st not keep,
My contemplation calls me, I must leave ye.

EDWIN: O reverent Sir, perswade not her to leave me.

HERMIT: My Lord I do not, nor to cease to love ye
I onely pray her faith may fixed stand,
Marriage was blest I know with heavens own hand.

(Exit HERMIT)

EDWIN: You hear him Lady, 'tis not a virgins state but sanctity of life, must make you happy.

MODESTIA: Good sir, you say you love me, gentle Edwin, even by that love I do beseech you leave me.

EDWIN: Think of your fathers tears, your weeping friends whom cruel grief makes pale and bloodless for you.

MODESTIA: Would I were dead to all.

EDWIN: Why do you weep?

MODESTIA: Oh who would live to see
How men with care and cost, seek misery.

EDWIN: Why do you seek it then? What joy, what pleasure, can give you comfort in a single life?

MODESTIA: The contemplation of a happy death, which is to me so pleasing that I think no torture could divert me: What's this world wherein you'd have me walk, but a sad passage to a dread Judgement Seat, from whence even now we are but bail'd, upon our good abearing, till that great Sessions come, when Death, the Cryer, will surely summon us, and all to appear, to plead us guilty or our bail to clear:

(Soft Musick)

## The Birth of Merlin

what musick's this?

(Enter two Bishops, EDWIN, DONOBERT, CLOSTER,
CADOR, CONSTANTIA, OSWOLD, TOCLIO)

EDWIN: Oh now resolve and think upon my love, this sounds the Marriage of your beauteous sister, vertuous Constantia, with the noble Cador, look, and behold this pleasure.

MODESTIA: Cover me with night, It is a vanity not worth the sight.

DONOBERT: See, see, she's yonder, pass on son Cador.
Daughter Constantia, I beseech you all unless she first move speech, salute her not. Edwin what good success?

EDWIN: Nothing as yet, unless this object take her.

DONOBERT: See, see, her eye is fixt upon her sister, seem careless all, and take no notice of her: on afore there, come my Constantia.

MODESTIA: Not speak to me, nor dain to cast an eye,
To look on my despised poverty?
I must be more charitable, pray stay lady, are not you she whom I did once call sister?

CONSTANTIA: I did acknowledge such a name to one whilst she was worthy of it, in whose folly since you neglect your fame and friends together,
In you I drown'd a sisters name for ever.

MODESTIA: Your looks did speak no less.

GLOSTER: It now begins to work, this fight has moved her.

DONOBERT: I know this trick would take, or nothing.

MODESTIA: Though you disdain in me a sisters name, yet charity me thinks should be so strong to instruct e're you reject, I am a wretch even follies instance, who perhaps have er'd, not having known the goodness bears so high and fair a show in you, which being exprest
I may recant this low despised life,
And please those friends whom I mov'd to grief.

CADOR: She is coming yfaith, be merry Edwin.

CONSTANTIA: Since you desire instruction you shall have it, what ist should make you thus desire to live vow'd to a single life?

MODESTIA: Because I know I cannot flie from death, oh my good sister, I beseech you hear me,
This world is but a Masque, catching weak eyes,
With what is not our selves but our disguise,
A Vizard that falls off, the Dance being done,

And leaves Deaths Glass for all to look upon,
Our best happiness here, lasts but a night,
Whose burning Tapers makes false Ware seem right;
Who knows not this, and will not now provide
Some better shift before his shame be spy'd,
And knowing this vain world at last will leave him,
Shake off these robes that help but to deceive him.

CONSTANTIA: Her words are powerful, I am amaz'd to hear her!

DONOBERT: Her soul's inchanted with infected Spells.
Leave her best Girl, for now in thee
Ile seek the fruits of Age, Posterity.
Out o'my fight; sure I was half asleep, or drunk when I begot thee.

CONSTANTIA: Good sir forbear. What say you to that sister?
The joy of children, a blest Mothers Name!
Oh who without much grief can loose such Fame?

MODESTIA: Who can enjoy it without sorrow rather?
And that most certain where the joy's unsure,
Seeing the fruit that we beget endure
So many miseries, that oft we pray
The Heavens to shut up their afflicted day:
At best we do but bring forth Heirs to die,
And fill the Coffins of our enemy.

CONSTANTIA: Oh my soul.

DONOBERT: Hear her no more Constantia, she's sure bewitcht with Error, leave her Girl.

CONSTANTIA: Then must I leave all goodness sir: away, stand off, I say.

DONOBERT: How's this?

CONSTANTIA: I have no father, friend, no husband now, all are but borrowed robes, in which we masque to waste and spend the time, when all our Life is but one good betwixt two Ague-days, which from the first, e're we have time to praise, a second Fever takes us: Oh my best sister, my souls eternal friend, forgive the rashness of my distemper'd tongue, for how could she knew not her self, know thy felicity, from which worlds cannot now remove me.

DONOBERT: Art thou mad too, fond woman? what's thy meaning?

CONSTANTIA: To seek eternal happiness in heaven, which all this world affords not.

CADOR: Think of thy Vow, thou art my promis'd Wife.

CONSTANTIA: Pray trouble me no further.

OMNES: Strange alteration!

CADOR: Why do you stand at gaze, you sacred Priests? you holy men be equal to the Gods, and consumate my Marriage with this woman.

BISHOP: Her self gives barr my Lord, to your desires, and our performance; 'tis against the Law and Orders of the Church to force a Marriage.

CADOR: How am I wrong'd! was this your trick, my Lord?

DONOBERT: I am abus'd past sufferance; grief and amazement strive which Sense of mine shall loose her being first; yet let me call thee Daughter.

CADOR: Me, Wife.

CONSTANTIA: Your words are air, you speak of want, to wealth,
And wish her sickness, newly rais'd to health.

DONOBERT: Bewitched Girls, tempt not an old mans fury, that hath no strength to uphold his feeble age, but what your fights give life to, oh beware, and do not make me curse you. Kneel.

MODESTIA: Dear father, here at your feet we kneel, grant us but this, that in your fight and hearing the good Hermit may plead our Cause; which if it shall not give such satisfaction as your Age desires, we will submit to you.

CONSTANTIA: You gave us life, save not our bodies, but our souls from death.

DONOBERT: This gives some comfort yet: Rise with my blessings.
Have patience, noble Cador, worthy Edwin, send for the Hermit that we may confer, for sure Religion tyes you not to leave
Your careful Father thus; if so it be,
Take you content, and give all grief to me.             (Exeunt)

    *Scene 3* (Thunder and Lightning, Enter DEVIL)

DEVIL: Mix light and darkness, earth and heaven dissolve, be of one piece agen, and turn to Chaos, break all your works you powers, and spoil the world, or if you will maintain earth still, give way and life to this abortive birth now coming, whose fame shall add unto your Oracles.
Lucina, Hecate, dreadful Queen of Night,
Bright Proserpine, be pleas'd for Ceres love,
From stigian darkness, summon up the Fates,
And in a moment bring them quickly hither,

Lest death do vent her birth and her together,
> (Thunder)

Assist you spirits of infernal deeps,
Squint ey'd Erictho, midnight Incubus.
Rise, rise to aid this birth prodigious.
> (Enter LUCINA, and the three FATES.)

DEVIL: Thanks Hecate, hail sister to the Gods, there lies your way, haste with the Fates, and help, Give quick dispatch unto her laboring throws, to bring this mixture of infernal seed to humane being
> (Exit FATES)

And to beguil her pains, till back you come,
Anticks shall dance and Musick fill the room.
> (Dance)

DEVIL: Thanks Queen of Shades.

LUCINA: Farewel, great servant to th'infernal King,
In honor of this childe, the Fates shall bring
All their assisting powers of Knowledge, Arts,
Learning, Wisdom, all the hidden parts
Of all-admiring Prophecy, to fore-see
The event of times to come, his Art shall stand
A wall of brass to guard the Brittain Land,
Even from this minute, all his Arts appears
Manlike in Judgement, Person, State, and years,
Upon his brest the Fates have fixt his name,
And since his birth place was this forrest here,
They now have nam'd him Merlin Silvester.

DEVIL: And Merlins name in Brittain shall live,
Whilst men inhabit here, or Fates can give,
Power to amazing wonder, envy shall weep,
And mischief sit and shake her ebbone wings,
Whilst all the world of Merlins magick sings.
> (Exit DEVIL and LUCINA)

*Scene 4* (Enter CLOWN)

CLOWN: Well, I wonder how my poor sister does, after all this thundering, I think she's dead, for I can hear no tidings of her. Those woods yields small comfort for her, I could meet nothing but a swinherds wife, keeping hogs by the Forestside, but neither she nor none of her sowes would stir a foot to help us; indeed I think she durst not trust her self amongst the trees with me, for I

## The Birth of Merlin

must needs confess I offer'd some kindness to her; well, I would fain know what's become of my sister, if she have brought me a yong Cousin, his face may be a picture to finde his Father by, so oh, sister Joan, Joan Go-too't where are thou?

(Within) JOAN: Here, here brother, stay but a while, I come to thee.

CLOWN: O brave, she's alive still, I know her voice, she speaks, and speaks cherfully methinks, how now, what Moon-calf has she got with her?

(Enter JOAN and MERLIN with a Book)

JOAN: Come my dear Merlin, why dost thou fix thine eye so deeply on that book?

MERLIN: To sound the depth of Arts, of Learning, Wisdom, Knowledge.

JOAN: Oh my dear, dear son, those studies fits thee when thou art a man.

MERLIN: Why mother, I can be but half a man at best,
And that is your mortality, the rest
In me is spirit, 'tis not meat, nor time,
That gives this growth and bigness, no, my years
Shall be more strange then yet my birth appears,
Look mother, there's my Uncle.

JOAN: How doest thou know him son, thou never saw'st him?

MERLIN: Yet I know him, and know the pains he has taken for ye, to finde out my Father, give me your hand, good Uncle.

CLOWN: Ha, ha, I'de laugh at that yfaith, do you know me sir?

MERLIN: Yes, by the same token that even now you kist the swinherds-wife 'ith' woods, and would have done more, if she would have let you, Uncle.

CLOWN: A witch, a witch, a witch, sister: rid him out of your company, he is either a witch or a conjurer, he could never have known this else.

JOAN: Pray love him brother, he is my son.

CLOWN: Ha, ha, this is worse then all the rest yfaith, by his beard he is more like your husband: let me see, is your great belly gone?

JOAN: Yes, and this the happy fruit.

CLOWN: What, this Hartichoke? A Childe born with a beard on his face?

JOAN GO-TOO'T AND HER SON MERLIN
Come my dear Merlin, why dost thou fix thine eye so deeply on that ban?

MERLIN: Yes, and strong legs to go, and teethe to eat.

CLOWN: You can nurse up your self then? There's some charges sav'd for Soap and Candle, 'slid I have heard of some that has been born with teeth, but never none with such a talking tongue before.

JOAN: Come, come, you must use him kindly brother, did you but know his worth,, you would make much of him.

CLOWN: Make much of a Moncky? This is worse then Tom Thumb, that let a fart in his Mothers belly, a Childe to speak, eat, and go the first hour of his birth, nay, such a Baby as had need of a Barber before he was born too; why sister this is monstrous, and shames all our kindred.

JOAN: That thus 'gainst nature and our common births, he comes thus furnisht to salute the world, is power of Fates, and gift of his great father.

CLOWN: Why, of what profession is your father sir?

MERLIN: He keeps a Hot-house 'ith' Low Countries, will you see him sir?

CLOWN: See him, why sister has the childe found his father?

MERLIN: Yes, and Ile fetch him Uncle.

(Exit MERLIN)

CLOWN: Do not Uncle me, till I know your kindred, for my conscience some Baboon begot thee, surely thou art horribly deceived sister, this Urchin cannot be of thy breeding, I shall be asham'd to call him cousin, though his father be a Gentleman.

(Enter MERLIN and DEVIL)

MERLIN: Now my kinde Uncle see,
The Childe has found his Father, this is he.

CLOWN: The devil it is, ha, ha, is this your sweet-heart sister? have we run through the Countrey, haunted the City, and examin'd the Court to finde out a Gallant with a Hat and Feather, and a silken Sword, and golden Hangers, and do you now bring me to a Ragamuffin with a face like a Frying-pan?

JOAN: Fie brother, you mistake, behold him better.

**THE DEVIL IN DISGUISE AS A GALLANT**
. . . and do you now bring me to a Ragamuffin with a face like a Frying-pan?

## The Birth of Merlin

CLOWN: How's this? do you juggle with me, or are mine eyes matches? Hat and Feather, Sword, and Hangers and all, this is a Gallant indeed sister, this has all the marks of him we look for.

DEVIL: And you have found him now sir? give me your hand, I now must call you brother.

CLOWN: Not till you have married my sister, for all this while she's but your whore, sir.

DEVIL: Thou art too plain, Ile satisfie that wrong to her, and thee, and all, with liberal hand: come, why art thou fearful?

CLOWN: Nay I am not afraid, and you were the devil, sir.

DEVIL: Thou needst not, keep with thy sister still, and Ile supply your wants, you shall lack nothing that gold and wealth can purchase.

CLOWN: Thank you brother, we have gone many a weary step to finde you; you may be a husband for a Lady, for you are far fetcht and dear bought, I assure you: Pray how should I call you son, my cousin here?

DEVIL: His name is Merlin.

CLOWN: Merlin! Your hand, cousin Merlin, for your fathers sake I accept you to my kindred: if you grow in all things as your Beard does, you will be talkt on. By your Mothers side cousin, you come of the Go-too'ts, Suffolk bred, but our standing house is at Hocklye i'th Hole, and Layton-buzzard. For your father, no doubt you may from him claim Titles of Worship, but I cannot describe it; I think his Ancestors came first from Hell-bree in Wales, cousin.

DEVIL: No matter whence we do derive our Name,
All Brittany shall ring of Merlin's fame,
And wonder at his acts. Go hence to Wales,
There live a while, there Vortiger the King
Builds Castles and strong Holds, which cannot stand
Unless supported by yong Merlins hand.
There shall thy fame begin, Wars are a breeding.
The Saxons practise Treason, yet unseen,
Which shortly shall break out: Fair Love, farewel,
Dear son and brother, here must I leave you all,
Yet still I will be near at Merlins call.

(Exit DEVIL)

MERLIN: Will you go Uncle?

CLOWN: Yes, Ile follow you, cousin: well, I do most horribly begin to suspect my kindred, this brother in law of mine is the Devil sure, and though he hide his horns with his Hat and Feather, I spi'd his cloven foot for all his cunning.

(Exit CLOWN)

Scene 5 (Enter OSTORIUS, OCTA, and PROXIMUS.)

OSTORIUS: Come, come, time calls our close Complots to action: go Proximus, with winged speed flie hence, hye thee to Wales, salute great Vortiger with these our Letters; bid the King to arms, tell him we have new friends, more Forces landed in Norfolk and Northumberland, bid him make haste to meet us; if he keep his word, wee'l part the Realm between us.

OCTA: Bend all thine Art to quit that late disgrace the Christian Hermit gave thee, make thy revenge both sure and home.

PROXIMUS: That thought sir, spurs me on, till I have wrought their swift destruction.

(Exit PROXIMUS)

OSTORIUS: Go then, and prosper. Octa, be vigilant: Speak, are the Forts possest? the Guards made sure? Revolve I pray on how large consequence the bare event and sequel of our hopes joyntly consists, that have embark't our lives upon the hazzard of the least miscarriage.

OCTA: All's sure, the Queen your sister hath contrived the cunning Plot so sure, as at an instant the Brothers shall be both surpriz'd and taken.

OSTORIUS: And both shall die, yet one a while must live, till we by him have gather'd strength and power to meet bold Edol their stern General, that now contrary to the Kings command, hath re-united all his cashier'd Troops, and this way beats his drums to threaten us.

OCTA: Then our Plot's discover'd.

OSTORIUS: Come, th'art a fool, his Army and his life is given unto us: where is the Queen, my sister?

OCTA: In conference with the Prince.

OSTORIUS: Bring the Guards nearer, all is fair and good,
Their Conference I hope shall end in blood.

(Exeunt)

**ARTESIA BETRAYS PRINCE UTER**
Enough: Help husband, king Aurelius, help, rescue betraid Artesia.

*Scene 6*   (Enter PRINCE and ARTESIA.)

ARTESIA: Come, come, you do but flatter, what you term love, is but a Dream of blood, wakes with enjoying, and with open eyes forgot, contemn'd, and lost.

PRINCE: I must be wary, her words are dangerous. True, we'l speak of Love no more then.

ARTESIA: Nay, if you will you may,
'Tis but in jest, and yet so children play
With fiery flames, and covet what is bright,
But feeling his effects, abhor the light.
Pleasure is like a Building, the more high,
The narrower still it grows, Cedars do dye
Soonest at top.

PRINCE: How does your instance suit?

ARTESIA: From Art and Nature to make sure the root,
And lay a fast foundation, e're I try
The incertain Changes of a wavering Skie.
Make you example thus – You have a kiss – was it not pleasing?

PRINCE: Above all name to express it.

ARTESIA: Yet now the pleasure's gone, and you have lost your joys possession.

PRINCE: Yet when you please this flood may ebb again.

ARTESIA: But where it never ebbs, there runs the main.

PRINCE: Who can attain such hopes?

ARTESIA: Ile show the way to it, give me a taste once more of what you may enjoy.
   (Kiss)

PRINCE: Impudent whore! I were more false than Atheism can be, Should I not call this high felicity.

ARTESIA: If I should trust your faith, alas I fear you soon would change belief.

PRINCE: I would covet Martyrdom to make't confirm'd.

ARTESIA: Give me your hand on that, you'l keep your word?

PRINCE: I will.

ARTESIA: Enough: Help husband, king Aurelius, help, rescue betraid Artesia.

PRINCE: Nay then 'tis I that am betraid I see,
Yet with thy blood Ile end thy Treachery.

ARTESIA: How now! what troubles you? Is this you sir, that but even now would suffer Martyrdom to win your hopes, and is there now such terror in names of men to fright you? nay then I see what mettle you are made on.

PRINCE: Ha! was it but tryal? then I ask your pardon: what a dull slave was I to be so fearful? Ile trust her now no more, yet try the utmost. I am resolved, no brother, no man breathing, were he my bloods begetter, should withhold me from your love, I'd leap into his bosom, and from his brest pull forth that happiness Heaven had reserved in you for my enjoying.

ARTESIA: I now you speak a Lover like a Prince: Treason, treason.

PRINCE: Agen?

ARTESIA: Help Saxon Princes: Treason!

  (Enter OSTORIUS, OCTA, etc.)

OSTORIUS: Rescue the Queen: strike down the Villain.

  (Enter EDOLL, AURELIUS, DONOBERT, CADOR, EDWIN, TOCLIO, OSWOLD, at the other door)

EDOL: Call in the Guards: the Prince in danger! Fall back dear Sir, my brest shall buckler you.

AURELIUS: Beat down their weapons.

EDOL: Slave, wert thou made of brass, my sword shall bite thee.

AURELIUS: Withdraw on pain of death: where is the Traitor?

ARTESIA: Oh save your life, my Lord, let it suffice my beauty forc't mine own captivity.

AURELIUS: Who did attempt to wrong thee?

PRINCE: Hear me, Sir.

AURELIUS: Oh my sad soul was't thou?

ARTESIA: Oh do not stand to speak, one minute stay, prevents a second speech for ever.

AURELIUS: Make our Guards strong: My dear Artesia, let us know thy wrongs, and our own dangers.

ARTESIA: The Prince your brother, with these Brittain Lords, have all agreed to take me hence by force, and marry me to him.

PRINCE: The Devil shall wed thee first: thy baseness and thy lust confound and rot thee.

ARTESIA: He courted me even now, and in mine ear sham'd not to plead his most dishonest love, and their attempts to seize your sacred person, either to shut you up within some prison, or which is worse, I fear to murther you.

OMNES BRITTAINS: 'Tis all as false as hell.

EDOL: And as foul as she is.

ARTESIA: You know me, Sir?

EDOL: Yes, Deadly Sin, we know you, and shall discover all your villany.

AURELIUS: Chester forbear.

OSTORIUS: Their treasons sir, are plain: Why are their Soldiers lodg'd so near the Court?

OCTA: Nay, why came he in arms so suddenly?

EDOL: You fleering Anticks, do not wake my fury.

OCTA: Fury!

EDOL: Ratsbane, do not urge me.

ARTESIA: Good sir, keep farther from them.

PRINCE: Oh my sick heart, she is a witch by nature, devil by art.

AURELIUS: Bite thine own slanderous tongue, 'tis thou art false, I have observ'd your passions long ere this.

OSTORIUS: Stand on your guard, my Lord, we are your friends, and all our Force is yours.

EDOL: To spoil and rob the Kingdom.

AURELIUS: Sir, be silent.

EDOL: Silent! how long? till Doomsday? shall I stand by, and hear mine Honor blasted with foul Treason, the State half lost, and your life endanger'd, yet be silent?

ARTESIA: Yes, my blunt Lord, unless you speak your Treasons. Sir, let your Guards, his Traitors, seize them all, and then let tortures and devulsive racks, force a Confession from them.

EDOL: Wilde-fire and Brimstone eat thee. Hear me sir.

AURELIUS: Sir, Ile not hear you.

EDOL: But you shall: Not hear me! Were the worlds Monarch, Caesar, living, he should hear me. I tell you Sir, these serpents have betraid your Life and Kingdom: does not every day bring tidings of more swarms of lowsie slaves, the offal fugitives of barren Germany, that land upon our Coasts, and by our neglect settled in Norfolk and Northumberland?

OSTORIUS: They come as Aids and Safeguards to the King.

OCTA: Has he not need, when Vortiger's in arms, and you raise Powers, 'tis thought, to joyn with him?

EDOL: Peace, you pernicious Rat.

DONOBERT: Prithee forbear.

EDOL: Away, suffer a gilded rascal, a low-bred despicable creeper, an insulting Toad, to spit his poison'd venome in my face!

OCTA: Sir, sir.

EDOL: Do not reply, you Cur, for by the Gods, tho' the Kings presence guard thee, I shall break all patience, and like a Lion rous'd to spoil, shall run foul-mouth'd upon thee, and devour thee quick. Speak sir, will you forsake these scorpions, or stay till they have stung you to the heart?

AURELIUS: Y'are traitors all, this is our wife, our Queen: brother Ostorius troop your Saxons up, we'l hence to Winchester, raise more powers, to man with strength the Castle Camilot: go hence false men, joyn you with Vortiger, the murderer of our brother Constantine: we'l hunt both him and you with dreadful vengance, Since Brittain fails, we'l trust to forrain friends,
And guard our person from your traitorous ends.

(Exeunt AURELIUS, OSTORIUS, OCTA, ARTESIA, TOCLIO, OSWOLD,)

EDWIN: He's sure bewitcht.

GLOSTER: What counsel now for safety?

DONOBERT: Onely this sir, with all the speed we can, preserve the person of the King and Kingdom.

CADOR: Which to effect, tis best march hence to Wales, and set on Vortiger before he joyn his Forces with the Saxons.

EDWIN: On then with speed for Wales and Vortiger, that tempest once o'reblown, we come Ostorius to meet thy traiterous Saxons, thee and them, that with advantage thus have won the King, to back your factions, and to work our ruines.
This by the Gods and my good Sword, I'le set
In bloody lines upon thy Burgonet.

(Exeunt)

# ACT IV.

*Scene 1*   (Enter CLOWN, MERLIN, and a little antick Spirit)

MERLIN: How now Uncle, why do you search your pockets so? do you miss anything?

CLOWN: Ha, Cousin Merlin, I hope your beard does not overgrow your honesty, I pray remember you are made up of sisters thread, I am mothers brother, whosoever was your father.

MERLIN: Why, wherein can you task my duty, Uncle?

CLOWN: Your self, or your page it must be, I have kept no other company, since your mother bound your head to my Protectorship, I do feel a fault of one side, either it was that Sparrowhawk, or a Cast of Merlins, for I finde a Covy of Cardecu's sprung out of my pocket.

MERLIN: Why, do you want any money Uncle? sirrah, had you any from him?

CLOWN: Deny it not, for my pockets are witness against you.

SPIRIT: Yes, I had, to teach you better wit to look to it.

CLOWN: Pray use your fingers better, and my wit may serve it is sir.

MERLIN: Well, restore it.

SPIRIT: There it is.

CLOWN: I, there's some honesty in this, 'twas a token from your invisible Father, Cousin, which I would not have to go invisibly from me agen.

MERLIN: Well, you are sure you have it now Uncle?

CLOWN: Yes, and mean to keep it now, from your pages filching fingers too.

SPIRIT: If you have it so sure, pray show it me agen.

CLOWN: Yes, my little juggler, I dare show it, ha, cleanly conveyance agen, ye have no invisible fingers have ye? 'Tis gone certainly.

SPIRIT: Why sir, I toucht you not.

MERLIN: Why look you Uncle, I have it now, how ill do you look to it? here keep it safer.

CLOWN: Ha, ha, this is fine yfaith, I must keep to me other company if you have these slights of hand.

## The Birth of Merlin

MERLIN: Come, come, Uncle, 'tis all my Art which shall not offend you sir, onely I give you a taste of it, to show you sport.

CLOWN: Oh, but 'tis ill jesting with a mans pocket tho' – but I am glad to see you cunning Cousin, for now will I warrant thee a living till thou diest. You have heard the news in Wales here?

MERLIN: Uncle, let me prevent your care and counsel, 'twill give you better knowledge of my cunning, you would prefer me now in hope of gain, to Vortiger King of the Welch Brittains, to whom are all the Artists summon'd now, that seeks the secrets of futurity: The Bards, the Druids, Wizards, Conjurers, not an Auralper with his Whistling spells, no Capuomanster with his musty fumes,
No Witch or Juggler, but is thither sent,
To calculate the strange and fear'd event
Of his prodigious Castle now in building,
Where all the labors of the painful day,
Are ruin'd still i'th night, and to this place you would have me go.

CLOWN: Well, if thy mother were not my sister, I would say she was a witch that begot this, but this is thy father, not thy mother wit, thou hast taken my tale into thy mouth and spake my thought before me, therefore away, shustle thy self amongst the Conjurers, and be a made man before thou comest to age.

MERLIN: Nay, but stay, Uncle, you overslip my dangers, the Prophecies and all the cunning Wizards, have certifi'd the King, that this his Castle can never stand, till the foundation's laid with Mortar temper'd with the fatal blood of such a childe, whose father was no mortal.

CLOWN: What's this to thee? If the devil were thy father, was not thy mother born at Carmarden? Diggon for that then, and then it must be a childes blood, and who will take thee for a childe with such a beard of thy face? Is there not diggon for that too Cousin?

MERLIN: I must not go, lend me your ear a while, I'le give you reasons to the contrary.

(Enter two Gentlemen)

1 GENTLEMAN: Sure this is an endless piece of work the King has sent us about!

2 GENTLEMAN: Kings may do it, man, the like has been done to finde out the Unicorn.

1 GENTLEMAN: Which will be sooner found I think, then this fien'd begotten childe we seek for.

2 GENTLEMAN: Pox of those Conjurers that would speak of such a

one, and yet all their cunning could not tell us where to finde him.

1 GENTLEMAN: In Wales they say assuredly he lives, come let's enquire further.

MERLIN: Uncle, your perswasions must not prevail with me, I know mine enemies better then you do.

CLOWN: I say th'art a bastard then if thou disobey thine Uncle, was not Joan Go-too't thy mother, my sister? if the devil were thy father, what kin art thou to any man alive, but Bailys and Brokers? and they are but brothers in Law in thee neither.

1 GENTLEMAN: How's this, I think we shall speed here.

2 GENTLEMAN: I, and unlook't for too, go ne're and listen to them.

CLOWN: Hast thou a beard to hide it, wil't thou show thy self a childe, wil't thou have more hair then wit? Wil't thou deny thy mother, because no body knows thy father? Or shall thine Uncle be an ass?

1 GENTLEMAN: Bless ye friend, pray what call you this small Gentlemans name?

CLOWN: Small, sir, a small man may be a great Gentleman, his father may be of an ancient house, for ought we know sir.

2 GENTLEMAN: Why? do you not know his father?

CLOWN: No, nor you neither I think, unless the devil be in ye.

1 GENTLEMAN: What is his name sir?

CLOWN: His name is my Cousin sir, his education is my sisters son, but his maners are his own.

MERLIN: Why ask ye Gentlemen? my name is Merlin.

CLOWN: Yes, and a Goshawk was his father, for ought we know, for I am sure his mother was a Windsucker.

2 GENTLEMAN: He has a mother then?

CLOWN: As sure as I have a sister, sir.

1 GENTLEMAN: But his father you leave doubtful.

CLOWN: Well Sir, as wise men as you, doubt whether he had a father or no?

1 GENTLEMAN: Sure this is he we seek for.

2 GENTLEMAN: I think no less: and sir, we let you know the King hath sent for you.

## The Birth of Merlin

CLOWN: The more childe he, and he had bin rul'd by me, he should have gone before he was sent for.

1 GENTLEMAN: May we not see his mother?

CLOWN: Yes, and feel her too if you anger her, a devilish thing I can tell ye she has been, Ile go fetch her to ye.

(Exit CLOWN)

2 GENTLEMAN: Sir, it were fit you did resolve for speed, you must unto the King.

MERLIN: My Service sir, shall need no strict command, it shall obey most peaceably, but needless 'tis to fetch what is brought home, my journey may be staid, the King is coming hither with the same quest you bore before him hark, this drum will tell ye.

(Within Drums beat a low March)

1 GENTLEMAN: This is some cunning indeed sir.

(Florish. Enter Vortiger reading a letter, Proximus, with Drum and Soldiers, etc.)

VORTIGER: Still in our eye your message Proximus, we keep to spur our speed: Ostorius, and Octa, we shall salute with succor against Prince Uter and Aurelius, whom now we hear incamps at Winchester, there's nothing interrupts our way so much, as doth the erection of this fatal Castle, that spite of all our Art and daily labor, the night still ruines.

PROXIMUS: As erst I did affirm, still I maintain, the fien'd begotten childe must be found out, whose blood gives strength to the foundation, it cannot stand else.

(Enter, CLOWN, JOAN and MERLIN)

VORTIGER: Ha! I'st so? then Proximus by this intelligence he should be found: speak, is this he you tell of?

CLOWN: Yes Sir, and I his Uncle, and she his mother.

VORTIGER: And who is his father?

CLOWN: Why, she his mother can best tell you that, and yet I think the childe be wise enough, for he has found his father.

VORTIGER: Woman, is this thy son?

JOAN: It is, my Lord.

VORTIGER: What was his father? Or where lives he?

MERLIN: Mother speak freely and unastonisht,
That which you dar'd to act, dread not to name.

JOAN: In which I shall betray my sin and shame, But since it must be so, then know great King, all that my self yet knows of him, is this: In pride of blood and beauty I did live, my glass the Altar was, my face the Idol, such was my peevish love unto my self, that I did hate all other, such disdain was in my scornful eye, that I suppos'd no mortal creature worthy to enjoy me.
Thus with the Peacock I beheld my train, but never saw the blackness of my feet, oft have I chid the winds for breathing on me, and curst the Sun, fearing to blast my beauty.
In midst of this most leaprous disease, a seeming fair yong man appear'd unto me, in all things suiting my aspiring pride, and with him brought along a conquering power,
To which my frailty yielded, from whose embraces
This issue came, what more he is, I know not.

VORTIGER: Some Incubus, or Spirit of the night begot him then, for sure no mortal did it.

MERLIN: No matter who my Lord, leave further quest, since 'tis as hurtful as unnecessary more to enquire: Go to the cause my Lord, why you have sought me thus?

VORTIGER: I doubt not but thou knowst, yet to be plain, I sought thee for thy blood.

MERLIN: By whose direction?

PROXIMUS: By mine, my Art infalable instructed me, upon thy blood must the foundation rise of the Kings building, it cannot stand else.

MERLIN: Hast thou such leisure to enquire my Fate, and let thine own hang careless over thee? Knowst thou what pendelous mischief roofs thy head, how fatal, and how sudden?

PROXIMUS: Pish, bearded abortive, thou foretel my danger! My Lord, he trifles to delay his own.

MERLIN: No, I yield my self: and here before the King, make good thine Augury, as I shall mine. If thy fate fall not, thou hast spoke all truth, and let my blood satisfie the Kings desires: if thou thy self wilt write thine Epitaph, dispatch it quickly, there's not a minutes time 'twixt thee and thy death.

(A stone falls and kills PROXIMUS)

PROXIMUS: Ha, ha, ha.

MERLIN: I, so thou mayest die laughing.

## The Birth of Merlin

VORTIGER: Ha! This is above admiration, look, is he dead?

CLOWN: Yes sir, here's brains to make morter on, if you'l use them: Cousin Merlin, there's no more of this stone fruit ready to fall, is there? I pray give your Uncle a little fair warning.

MERLIN: Remove that shape of death, and now my Lord for clear satisfaction of your doubts, Merlin will show the fatal cause that keeps your fatal Castle down, and hinders your proceedings. Stand there, and by an apparition see the labor and end of all your destiny . . . Mother and Uncle, you must be absent.

CLOWN: Is your father coming Cousin?

MERLIN: Nay, you must be gone.

JOAN: Come, you'l offend him brother.

CLOWN: I would fain see my Brother i'law, if you were married I might lawfully call him so.

    (MERLIN strikes his wand. Thunder and lightning, two Dragons appear, a White and a Red, they fight a while and pause).

VORTIGER: What means this stay?

MERLIN: Be not amaz'd my Lord, for on the victory
Of loss or gain, as these two Champions ends
Your fate, your life, and kingdom all depends, therefore observe it well.

VORTIGER: I shall, heaven be auspicious to us.

    (Thunder: The Two Dragons fight again, and the White Dragon drives off the Red)

VORTIGER: The conquest is on the white Dragons part, now Merlin faithfully expound the meaning.

MERLIN: Your Grace must then not be offended with me.

VORTIGER: It is the weakest part I found in thee, to doubt of me so slightly, shall I blame my prophet that foretells me of my dangers? Thy cunning I approve most excellent.

MERLIN: Then know my Lord, there is a dampish Cave, the nightly habitation of these Dragons, vaulted beneath where you would build your Castle, whose enmity and nightly combats there, maintain a constant ruine of your labors: To make it more plain, the Dragons then yourself betoken, and the Saxon King, the vanquisht Red, is sir, your dreadful Emblem.

**MERLIN CONJURES DRAGONS FOR KING UTER**
  Be not amaz'd my Lord, for on the victory
  Of loss or gain, as these two Champions ends
  Your fate, your life, and kingdom all depends,
  therefore observe it well.

VORTIGER: Oh my fate!

MERLIN: Nay, you must hear with patience Royal sir, you slew the lawful King Constantius, 'twas a red deed, your Crown his blood did cement, the English Saxon first brought in by you, for aid against Constantius brethren, is the white horror who now knit together, have driven and shut you up in these wilde mountains; and though they now seek to unite with friendship, it is to wound your bosom, not embrace it, and with an utter extirpation to rout the Brittains out, and plant the English. Seek for your safety Sir, and spend no time to build the airy Castles, for Prince Uter armed with vengeance for his brothers blood is hard upon you, if you mistrust me, and to my words craves witness sir, then know here comes a messenger to tell you so.

(Exit MERLIN. Enter MESSENGER)

MESSENGER: My lord! Prince Uter!

VORTIGER: And who else sir?

MESSENGER: Edol, the great General.

VORTIGER: The great Devil, they are coming to meet us.

MESSENGER: With a full power my Lord.

VORTIGER: With a full vengeance they mean to meet us, so! We are ready to their confront At full march double footing, we'l loose no ground, nor shall their numbers fright us,
If it be Fate, it cannot be withstood.
We got our Crown so, be it lost in blood.

(Exeunt)

Scene 2  (Enter PRINCE UTER, EDOL, CADOR, EDWIN, TOCLIO, with Drum and Soldiers)

PRINCE: Stay, and advice, hold drum.

EDOL: Beat slave, why do you pause? why make a stand? where are our enemies? or do you mean we fight amongst our selves?

PRINCE: Nay, noble Edol, let us here take counsel, it cannot hurt, it is the surest Garison to safety.

EDOL: Fie on such slow delays! so fearful men that are to pass over a flowing river, stand on the bank to parly of the danger, till the tide rise, and then be swallowed. Is not the King in field?

CADOR: Proud Vortiger, the Trator is in field.

EDWIN: The Murderer, and Usurper.

EDOL: Let him be the devil so I might fight with him, for heavens love sir march on, oh my patience, will you delay untill the Saxons come to aid his party?

    (A Tucket)

PRINCE: There's no such fear, prithee be calm a while, hark, it seems by this, he comes or sends to us.

EDOL: If it be for parly, I will drown the summons, if all our drums and hoarseness choke me not.

    (Enter Captain)

PRINCE: Nay, prithee hear, from whence art thou?

CAPTAIN: From the King Vortiger.

EDOL: Traitor, there's none such: Alarum drum, strike slave, or by mine honor I will break thy head, and beat thy drums heads both about thine ears.

PRINCE: Hold noble Edol, let's hear what Articles he can inforce.

EDOL: What articles, or what conditions can you expect to value half your wrong, unless he kill himself by thousand tortures, and send his carcase to appease your vengeance, for the foul murder of Constantius, and that's not a tenth part neither.

PRINCE: 'Tis true, my brothers blood is crying to me now, I do appaud thy counsel: hence, be gone.

                                              (Exit Captain)

We'l hear no parly now but by our swords.

EDOL: And those shall speak home in death killing words, Alarum to the fight, sound, sound the Alarum.

                                                    (Exeunt)

    Scene 3    (Alarum Enter EDOL driving all Vortigers Force before him, then Enter PRINCE UTER pursuing VORTIGER)

VORTIGER: Dost follow me?

PRINCE: Yes, to thy death I will.

VORTIGER: Stay, be advis'd, I would not be the onely fall of Princes, I slew thy brother.

PRINCE: Thou didst black Traitor, and in that vengeance I pursue thee.

VORTIGER: Take mercy for thy self, and flie my sword, save

## The Birth of Merlin

thine own life as satisfaction, which here I give thee for thy brothers death.

PRINCE: Give what's thine own: a Traitors heart and head, that's all thou art right Lord of; the Kingdom which thou usurp'st, thou most unhappy Tyrant, is leaving thee, the Saxons which thou broughtst to back thy usurpations, are grown great, and where they seat themselves, do hourly seek to blot the Records of old Brute and Brittains, from memory of men, calling themselves Hingest-men, and Hingest-land, that no more the Brittain name be known; all this by thee, thou base destroyer of thy Native Countrey.

(Enter EDOL)

EDOL: What, stand you talking? Fight.

PRINCE: Hold Edol.

EDOL: Hold out my sword, and listen not to King or Princes word, There's work enough abroad, this task is mine.

(Alarum)

PRINCE: Prosper thy Valour, as thy Vertues shine.

(Exeunt)

*Scene 4* (Enter CADOR and EDWIN)

CADOR: Bright Victory her self fights on our part, and buckled in a golden Beaver, rides triumphantly before us.

EDWIN: Justice is with her, who ever takes the true and rightful cause, let us not lag behinde them.

(Enter PRINCE)

CADOR: Here comes the Prince, how goes our fortunes Sir?

PRINCE: Hopeful, and fair, brave Cador, proud Vortiger beat down by Edols sword, was rescu'd by the following multitudes, and now for safety's fled unto a Castle here standing on the hill: but I have sent a cry of hounds as violent as hunger,
To break his stony walls, or if they fail,
We'l send in wilde fire to dislodge him thence,
Or burn them all with flaming violence.

(Exeunt)

*Scene 5* (Blazing Star appears. Florish Tromp.
Enter PRINCE, UTER, EDOL, CADOR, EDWIN, TOCLIO with Drum and Soldiers)

PRINCE: Look Edol: Still this fiery exalation shoots his frightful horrors on th'amazed world, see in the beam that 'bout his flaming

**THE COMET REVEALS THE DEATH OF KINGS**
Look Edol: Still this fiery exalation shoots his frightful horrors on th'amazed world...

## The Birth of Merlin

ring, a Dragons head appears, from out whose mouth two flaming snakes of fire, stretch East and West.

EDOL: And see, from forth the body of the Star, seven smaller blazing streams, directly point on this affrighted kingdom.

CADOR: 'Tis a dreadful Meteor.

EDWIN: And doth portend strange fears.

PRINCE: This is no Crown of Peace, this angry fire hath something more to burn then Vortiger; if it alone were pointed at his fall, it would pull in his blasing Piramids, and be appeas'd, for Vortiger is dead.

EDOL: These never come without their large effects.

PRINCE: The will of heaven be done, our sorrows this, we want, a mistick Pithon to expound this fiery Oracle.

CADOR: Oh no my Lord, you have the best that ever Brittain bred, and durst I prophecy of your Prophet, sir, none like him shall suceed him.

PRINCE: You mean Merlin.

CADOR: True sir, wonderous Merlin, he met us in the way, and did foretell the fortunes of this day successful to us.

EDWIN: He's sure about the Camp, send for him sir.

CADOR: He told the bloody Vortiger his fate, and truely too, and if I could give faith to any Wizards skill, it should be Merlin.

(Enter MERLIN and CLOWN)

CADOR: And see my Lord, as if to satisfie your Highness pleasure, Merlin is come.

PRINCE: See, the Comet's in his eye, disturb him not.

EDOL: With what a piercing judgement he beholds it!

MERLIN: Whither will Heaven and Fate translate this Kingdom?
What revolutions, rise and fall of Nations
Is figur'd yonder in that Star, that sings
The change of Brittains State, and death of Kings?
Ha! He's dead already, how swiftly mischief creeps!
Thy fatal end sweet Prince, even Merlin weeps.

PRINCE: He does foresee some evil, his action shows it, for e're he does expound, he weeps the story.

EDOL: There's another weeps too. Sirrah dost thou understand what thou lamentst for?

CLOWN: No sir, I am his Uncle, and weep because my Cousin

weeps, flesh and blood cannot forbear.

PRINCE: Gentle Merlin, speak thy prophetick knowledge, in explanation of this fiery horror, from which we gather from thy mournful tears, much sorrow and disaster in it.

MERLIN: 'Tis true fair Prince, but you must hear the rest with patience.

PRINCE: I vow I will, tho' it portend my ruine.

MERLIN: There's no such fear, this brought the fiery fall of Vortiger, and yet not him alone, this day is faln a King more good, the glory of our Land, the milde, and gentle sweet Aurelius.

PRINCE: Our brother!

EDWIN: Forefend it heaven.

MERLIN: He at his Palace Royal sir at Winchester, this day is dead and poison'd.

CADOR: By whom? Or what means Merlin?

MERLIN: By the Traiterous Saxons.

EDOL: I ever fear'd as much: that devil Ostorius, and the damn'd witch Artesia, sure has done it.

PRINCE: Poison'd! oh look further gentle Merlin, behold the Star agen, and do but finde revenge for me, though it cost thousand lives, and mine the foremost.

MERLIN: Comfort yourself, the heavens have given it fully, all the portentious ills to you is told, now hear a happy story sir from me, to you and to your fair posterity.

CLOWN: Me thinks I see something like a peel'd Onion, it makes me weep agen.

MERLIN: Be silent Uncle, you'l be forc't else.

CLOWN: Can you not finde in the Star, Cousin, whether I can hold my tongue or no?

EDOL: Yes, I must cut it out.

CLOWN: Phu, you speak without book sir, my Cousin Merlin knows.

MERLIN: True, I must tie it up, now speak your pleasure Uncle.

CLOWN: Hum, hum, hum, hum.

MERLIN: So, so – now observe my Lord, and there behold above yon flame-hair'd beam that upward shoots, appears a Dragons head, out of whose mouth two streaming lights point their flam-feather'd darts contrary ways, yet both shall have their aims:
Again behold from the ignifirent body, seven splendant and illustrious

## The Birth of Merlin

rays are spred, all speaking Heralds to this Brittain Isle, and thus they are expounded:

The Dragons head is the Herogliphick that figures out your Princely self, that here must reign a King, those by-form'd fires that from the Dragons mouth shoot East and West, emblem two Royal babes, which shall proceed from you, a son and daughter.

Her pointed constellation Northwest bending,

Crowns Her a Queen in Ireland, of whom first springs

That Kingdoms Title to the Brittain Kings.

CLOWN: Hum, hum, hum.

MERLIN: But of your Son, thus Fate and Merlin tells, all after times shall fill their Chronicles with fame of his renown, whose warlike sword shall pass through fertile France and Germany; nor shall his conjuring foot be forc't to stand, till Romes Imperial Wreath hath crown'd his Fame with Monarch of the West, from whose seven hills, with Conquest, and contributory Kings, he back returns to inlarge the Brittain bounds, his Heraldry adorn'd with thirteen Crowns.

CROWN: Hum, hum, hum.

MERLIN: He to the world shall add another Worthy, and as a Loadstone for his prowess, draw a train of Marshal Lovers to his Court: It shall be then the best of Knight-hoods honor, at Winchester to fill his Castle Hall, and at his Royal Table sit and feast in warlike orders, all their arms round hurl'd, as if they meant to circumscribe the world.

(He touches the Clowns mouth with his wand)

CLOWN: Hum, hum, hum, oh that I could speak a little.

MERLIN: I know your mind Uncle, agen be silent.

(Strikes again)

PRINCE: Thou speakst of wonders Merlin, prithee go on, declare at full this Constellation.

MERLIN: Those seven beams pointing downward, sir, betoken the troubles of this Land, which then shall meet with other Fate: War and Dissension strives to make division, till seven Kings agree to draw this Kingdom to a Hepterchy.

PRINCE: Thine art hath made such proof, that we believe thy words authentical, be ever neer us, my Prophet, and the Guide of all my actions.

MERLIN: My service shall be faithful to your person, and all my studies for my Countries safety.

CLOWN: Hum, hum, hum.

MERLIN: Come, you are releast, sir.

CLOWN: Cousin, pray help me to my tongue agen, you do not mean I shall be dumb still I hope?

MERLIN: Why, hast thou not thy tongue?

CLOWN: Ha! yes, I feel it now, I was so long dumb, I could not well tell whether I spake or no.

PRINCE: I'st thy advice we presently pursue the bloody Saxons, that have slain my brother?

MERLIN: With your best speed, my Lord, Prosperity will keep you company.

CADOR: Take then your Title with you, Royal Prince, 'twill adde unto our strength, Long Live King Uter.

EDOL: Put the Addition to't that Heaven hath given you: The DRAGON is your Emblem, bear it bravely, and so long live and ever happy styl'd Uter-Pendragon, lawful King of Brittain.

PRINCE: Thanks Edol, we imbrace the name and title, and in our Shield and Standard shall the figure of a Red Dragon still be born before us, to fright the bloody Saxons. Oh my Aurelius,
Sweet rest thy soul; let thy disturbed spirit
Expect revenge, think what it would, it hath,
The Dragon's coming in his fiery wrath.

(Exeunt)

**UTER PENDRAGON KING OF BRITTAIN**
The DRAGON is your Emblem, bear it bravely, and so long live and ever happy styl'd Uter-Pendragon, lawful King of Brittain.

# ACT V

*Scene 1*  (Thunder, then Music: Enter JOAN fearfully, the DEVIL following her)

JOAN: Hence thou black horror, is thy lustful fire kindled agen? not thy loud throated thunder, nor thy adulterate infernal Musick, shall e're bewitch me more, oh too too much is past already.

DEVIL: Why dost thou fly me? I come a Lover to thee, to imbrace, and gently twine thy body in mine arms.

JOAN: Out thou Hell-hound.

DEVIL: What hound so e're I be,
Fawning and sporting as I would with thee,
why should I not be stroakt and plaid withal, will't
thou not thank the Lion might devour thee, if he
shall let thee pass?

JOAN: Yes, thou art he, free me, and Ile thank thee.

DEVIL: Why, whither wouldst? I am at home with thee, thou art mine own, have we not charge of family together, where is your son?

JOAN: Oh darkness cover me.

DEVIL: There is a pride which thou hast won by me, the mother of a fame shall never die, kings shall have need of written Chronicles, to keep their names alive, but Merlin none:
Ages to ages shall like Sabalists
Report the wonders of his name and glory,
While there are tongues and times to tell his story.

JOAN: Oh rot my memory before my flesh, let him be called some hell or earth-bred monster, that ne're had hapless woman for a mother; sweet death deliver me, hence from my sight, why shouldst thou now appear? I had no pride nor lustful thought about me, to conjure and call thee to my ruine, when as at first thy cursed person became visible.

DEVIL: I am the same I was.

JOAN: But I am chang'd.

DEVIL: Agen Ile change thee to the same thou wert, quench to my lust, come forth by thunder led, my Coajutors in the spoils of mortals.

(Thunder. Enter Spirit)

Claspe in your Ebon arms that prize of mine, mount her as high as palled Hecate; and on this rock Ile stand to cast up fumes and darkness o're the blew fac'd firmament; from Brittain, and from Merlin, Ile remove her, they ne're shall meet agen.

JOAN: Help me some saving hand, if not too late, I cry let mercy come.

(Enter MERLIN)

MERLIN: Stay you black slaves of night, let loose your hold, set her down safe, or by th'infernal Stix, Ile binde you up with exorcisms so strong that all the black pentagoron of hell shall ne're release you. Save your selves and vanish.

(Exit Spirit)

DEVIL: Ha! What's he?

MERLIN: The Childe has found his Father, do you not know me?

DEVIL: Merlin!

JOAN: Oh, help me gentle son.

MERLIN: Fear not, they shall not hurt you.

DEVIL: Relievest thou her to disobey thy father?

MERLIN: Obedience is no lesson in your school: nature and kind to her commands my duty, the part that you begot was against kinde, so all I ow to you is to be unkind.

DEVIL: Ile blast thee slave to death, and on this rock stick thee an eternal monument.

MERLIN: Ha, ha, thy powers too weak, what art thou devil, but an inferior lustful Incubus, taking advantage of the wanton flesh, wherewith thou dost beguile the ignorant? put off the form of thy humanity, and cral upon thy speckled belly, serpent, or Ile unclap the jaws of Achoron and fix thee ever in the local fire.

DEVIL: Traitor to hell; curse that I e're begot thee.

MERLIN: Thou didst beget thy scourge, storm not, not stir, the power of Merlins Art is all confirm'd in the Fates decretals, – Ile ransack hell, and make thy

(Thunder and Lightning in the Rock)

masters bow unto my spells, thou first shall taste it, – Tenibrarum precis, devitiarum, and infirorum, Deus, hunc Incubum in ignis eterni abisum accipite, aut in hoc carcere tenebroso, in sempeternum astringere mando.

(The Rock encloses him)

So, there beget earthquakes or some noisom damps, for never shalt thou touch a woman more: How chear you mother?

JOAN: Oh now my son is my deliverer, yet I must name him with my deepest sorrow.

(Alarum afar off)

MERLIN: Take comfort now, past times are ne're recal'd, I did foresee your mischief and prevent it: hark, how the sounds of war now call me hence to aid Pendragon, that in battail stands against the Saxons, from whose aid Merlin must not be absent. Leave this soyl, and Ile conduct you to a place retir'd, which I by art have rais'd, call'd Merlins Bower, there shall you dwell with solitary sighs, with grones and passions your companions, to weep away this flesh you have offended with, and leave all bare unto your aierial soul:

And when you die, I will erect a Monument upon the verdant Plains of Salisbury, no King shall have so high a sepulchre, with pendulous stones that I will hang by art, where neither Lime nor Morter shalbe us'd, a dark Enigma to the memory, for none shall have the power to number them, a place that I will hollow for your rest, Where no Night-hag shall walk, nor Ware-wolf tread, Where Merlins Mother shall be sepulcher'd.

(Exeunt)

Scene 2   (Enter DONOBERT, GLOSTER and HERMIT)

DONOBERT: Sincerely Gloster, I have told you all. My Daughters are both vow'd to Single Life, and this day gone unto the Nunnery, though I begot them to another end, and fairly promis'd them in Marriage, one to Earl Cador, t'other to your son, my worthy friend, the Earl of Gloster. Those lost, I am lost: they are lost, all's lost. Answer me this then, Ist a sin to marry?

HERMIT: Oh no, my Lord.

DONOBERT: Go to then, Ile go no further with you, I perswade you to no ill, perswade you then that I perswade you well.

GLOSTER: 'Twill be a good Office in you, sir.

(Enter CADOR and EDWIN)

**MERLIN BANISHES HIS FATHER INTO A ROCK**
So, there beget earthquakes or some noisom damps, for never shalt thou touch a woman more. . .

*The Childe hath found his Father*

DONOBERT: Which since they thus neglect, my memory shall lose them now for ever. See, see the Noble Lords, their promis'd Husbands! had Fate so pleas'd, you might have call'd me Father.

EDWIN: Those hopes are past, my Lord, for even this minute we saw them both enter the Monastery, secluded from the world and men for ever.

CADOR: 'Tis both our griefs we cannot, Sir, but from the King take you the Times joy from us; The Saxon King Ostorius slain, and Octa fled, that Woman-fury, Queen Artesia, is fast in hold, and forc't to re-deliver London and Winchester (which she had fortifi'd) to Princely Uter, lately styl'd Pendragon, who now triumphantly is marching hither to be invested with the Brittain Crown.

DONOBERT: The joy of this, shall banish from my breast all thought that I was Father to two Children, two stubborn Daughters, that have left me thus. Let my old arms embrace, and call you Sons; for by the Honor of my Fathers House, I'le part my estate most equally betwixt you.

EDWIN, CADOR: Sir, y'are most noble!

(Flor. Tromp. Enter EDOL with Drum and Colours, OSWOLD bearing the Standard, TOCLIO the Sheild, with the Red Dragon pictur'd in 'em, two Bishops with the Crown, PRINCE UTER, MERLIN, ARTESIA bound, Guard and CLOWN)

PRINCE: Set up our Sheild and Standard, noble Soldiers, We have firm hope that tho' our Dragon sleep, Merlin will us and our fair Kingdom keep.

CLOWN: As his Uncle lives, I warrant you.

GLOSTER: Happy Restorer of the Brittains fame, uprising Sun let us salute thy glory, ride in a day perpetual about us, and no night be in thy thrones zodiack, why do we stay to binde those Princely browes with this Imperial Honor?

PRINCE: Stay noble Gloster, that monster first must be expel'd our eye, or we shall take no joy in it.

DONOBERT: If that be hindrance, give her quick Judgement, and send her hence to death, she has long deserv'd it.

EDOL: Let my Sentence stand for all, take her hence, and stake her carcase in the burning Sun, till it be parcht and dry, and then fley off her wicked skin, and stuff the pelt with straw to be shown up and down at Fairs and Markets, two pence a piece to see so foul a Monster, will be a fair Monopoly and worth the begging.

## The Birth of Merlin

ARTESIA: Ha, ha, ha.

EDOL: Dost laugh Erictho?

ARTESIA: Yes, at thy poor invention, is there no better, torture-monger?

DONOBERT: Burn her to dust.

ARTESIA: That's a Phoenix death, and glorious.

EDOL: I, that's to good for her.

PRINCE: Alive she shall be buried circled in a wall, thou murdress of a King, there starve to death.

ARTESIA: Then Ile starve death when he comes for his prey, and i'th' mean time Ile live upon your curses.

EDOL: I, 'tis diet good enough, away with her.

ARTESIA: With joy, my best of wishes is before,
They brother's poison'd, but I wanted more.

(Exit)

PRINCE: Why does our Prophet Merlin stand apart, sadly observing these our Ceremonies, and not applaud our joys with thy hid knowledge? Let thy divining Art now satisfie some part of my desires, for well I know 'tis in thy power to show the full event, that shall both end our Reign and Chronicle: speak learned Merlin, and resolve my fears, whether by war we shall expel the Saxons, or govern what we hold with beauteous peace in Wales and Brittain?

MERLIN: Long happiness attend Pendragons Reign, what Heaven decrees, fate hath no power to alter: The Saxons, sir, will keep the ground they have, and by supplying numbers still increase, till Brittain be no more. So please your Grace, I will in visible apparitions, present you Prophecies which shall concern Succeeding Princes, which my Art shall raise, Till men shall call these times the latter days.

PRINCE: Do it my Merlin, and Crown me with much joy and wonder.

(MERLIN strikes. Hoeboys, Enter a King in Armour, his Shield quartered with thirteen Crowns. At the other door enter divers Princes who present their Crowns to him at his feet, and do him homage, then enters Death and strikes him, he growing sick, Crowns Constantine. Exeunt)

MERLIN: This King, my Lord, presents your Royal Son, who in his prime of years shall be so fortunate, that thirteen several Princes shall present their several Crowns unto him, and all Kings else shall so admire his fame and victories, that they shall be glad either through fear or love, to do him homage; but death (who neither favors the weak nor valliant) in the middest of all his glories, soon shall seize him, scarcely permitting him to appoint one in all his purchased Kingdoms to succeed him.

PRINCE: Thanks to our Prophet for this so wish'd for satisfaction, and hereby now we learn that always Fate must be observ'd, what ever that decree,
All future times shall still record this Story,
Of Merlin's learned worth, and Arthur's glory.

(Exeunt Omnes)

FINIS